# About the author

Lindsay Leigh is a child practitioner who became a foster carer for her local authority in 2013 to an eight-week-old baby boy. She had no idea of what was to come but kept on fighting the system. She later gained qualifications in child psychology, mental health, foetal alcohol spectrum disorders (FASD), and other disabilities, all to help the little boy she cared for. She left no stone unturned and is still to this day battling for him and other families who have children with FASD. Lindsay Leigh now lives in a new location away from the local authority that she fostered for with her husband and three children. She runs a small support group for other carers and has started university to study counselling. This is her first book.

# SOCIAL INJUSTICE

# LINDSAY LEIGH

## SOCIAL INJUSTICE

Vanguard Press

A CIP catalogue record for this title is
available from the British Library.

ISBN 978 1 80016 147 4

*Vanguard Press is an imprint of
Pegasus Elliot MacKenzie Publishers Ltd.*
www.pegasuspublishers.com

First Published in 2021

**Vanguard Press
Sheraton House Castle Park
Cambridge England**

Printed & Bound in Great Britain

All names and locations have been changed to protect
the identity of the real-life characters.

He goes by the name of 'live wire'
Runs like the wind, swings like a monkey, talks like a parrot.
He has no filter, no impulse control.
He bounces off the wall like a bouncy ball, gets up and down like a yoyo.
He's a colourful character, yet a black and white thinker.
Everything is straight to the point.
He leaves people open mouthed, stunned into silence.
Living with him is like being on a rollercoaster that runs for miles and miles.
Ups and downs but not many straight lines.
His batteries never run down, just a small break at night to recharge.
He gives Buzz Lightyear a run for his money.
He is a six a.m. alarm that rings sharp and loud, piercing eardrums for miles.
With big blue eyes and soft brown hair, a thin upper lip, button nose and a flat midface, he melts hearts.
His mischievous face lights the room like a firework display and brings out the smiles in others.
He is wired differently from the poison of alcohol dripped into his forming brain.
He has a heart of gold and warms the hearts of all those around him, opening eyes and pulling them into his world.

For you, Grandad

# Prologue

I awake to a loud bang on the door. It's still dark and for a minute I'm wondering where I am and what is happening. I slowly rise out of bed when the banging becomes louder and more insistent. I rush down the stairs half asleep, tripping on the bottom step. Peeking through the spyhole in the door I can see a police uniform and I can hear walkie talkies sounding in the background. *What on earth is going on?* I think, startled. I slowly open the door. Two male police officers and a small lady with short bobbed mousy brown hair stand on the black doormat, looking at me.

"Is everything okay?" I ask, confused.

I'm quickly cut off. The police officers, barge past me, stopping at the stairs with the small lady following behind. One of the male police officers says abruptly, "We have a court order to take Chase Groves back into the care of the local authority."

"What on earth for?" I demand, panic-stricken.

The woman is wearing a navy-blue suit with a name badge that I can't quite make out. I rub the sleep from my eyes and then it hits me, she must be a social worker from the local authority. She sniggers and barges past me, heading for the stairs. As I look up, I see Debbie standing at the top in her bright pink princess pyjamas, tears streaming down her innocent little face.

"Please don't take my baby brother!" she cries. "We only want to look after him. We love him!"

The woman races upstairs, barging past Debbie who looks terrified, and heads straight into the bedroom. She starts lifting Chase from his bed. Running up the stairs after her, I try to grab Chase from her.

"*Get off him*!" I scream. "Why are you doing this to us?"

She's got a firm grip of him and he's starting to stir. "Mummmmmyyyyyy!" he says sleepily, opening his eyes.

"*You can't do this!*" I scream, and then I jolt up, shaking, wide awake. I turn to my side to see Chase fast asleep next to me with the dull light from the landing shining in. The alarm clock lights up from across the room. *It's three thirty a.m.* I look up at the dark ceiling, in a cold sweat, and with a heavy breath let out a big sigh of relief.

# Where it all began — Three years earlier

Feeling nervous, I step out of the car, looking around before picking up the empty car seat from the back leather chair. I've known for some time that this day would eventually come. I hadn't expected it to happen quite like this, though. Four months ago, I had met with a social worker and started the assessments needed to be approved as a foster carer for the local authority. Although I understood that they had to be thorough, the process was a lot lengthier and more intrusive than I had been led to believe. I had done a family tree, spoken about my childhood, the schools I had attended, and I had even had to tell them which contraception I was on. I had to have further background checks as well as giving them access to my personal medical history.

"They make fostering sound so easy, don't they?" I laughed to my mum one day. When I first saw it advertised on all the big posters in town, it had simply said: *Could you foster? Do you have a spare room?* There had been a lot of advertising on the internet and billboards around town suggesting that you could earn up to five hundred pounds a week. The pay turned out to be just ninety pounds a week carer's allowance plus the child's weekly allowance to cover all items and general care costs. None of this had put me off, though. Fresh out of college and newly qualified as a child practitioner, I had wanted a challenging new career that was different and rewarding too. I also didn't want to be away from my daughter Debbie who had just turned four in June. Fostering just seemed perfect.

So here I stand, waiting anxiously outside of the court, ready to walk in and collect an eight-week-old baby boy from his parents. I only got approved at a panel just three days ago and have not been given the grant money yet to go out and buy all of the items he needs. After getting the phone call this morning, I rushed out in a panic with the only money I had available and quickly picked up the cheapest pushchair, Moses basket, and accessories I could find.

I can feel the glares cutting into me as I walk through the court foyer, heading towards security. I find myself constantly looking behind me for any sign of angry parents, although, of course, I have no idea what his parents even look like. I secretly hope his mum and dad will be mad at me. I think I will find it harder if they are upset and crying. I will have less sympathy for taking the baby off them if they are aggressive in front of him. I still can't see any sign of the child's social worker who is meant to be meeting me here. Surely, he should be looking out for me?

"Can I help you?" a large female security guard with spikey bright red hair says now. I feel panic as I suddenly realize that I haven't even received the ID badge that I should have been carrying with me for situations like this. Hopefully, she won't ask.

"Hi, I'm a local authority foster carer…" I begin to explain. "I have been sent here by children's services to pick up a baby boy. His name is Chase Groves. I'm meeting the child's social worker here. His name is Robert. He's in his mid to late thirties, dark hair, large build. I'm unsure of his surname." She suddenly goes straight-faced and gives me a look that I can't quite work out.

"Back room now!" she orders. "If you are talking about the parents that I think you are, then I suggest you stay in there with security." She glances over and nods at the other two security guards, who then escort me to a small back room just before the main front doors.

The female security guard then walks through the doors mumbling something about finding out what is going on.

I stand in the room, the security guards in front of the door. They close it slightly, and I suddenly feel claustrophobic. It feels like a lifetime later before the female security guard returns. "I'm afraid the child's social worker has left the court after an altercation with the baby's father. He's been quite aggressive towards the social workers today, especially Robert, but he's gone now after storming out and kicking that bin outside." She points towards the door. "Mother and baby are through the double doors and to your right in the family room with another social worker, I've been told. Come with me, and I will take you through." She walks, and I follow.

"Have you collected children like this before?" she asks.

"No," I say. "It's my first day. I only got approved as a local authority foster carer the other day."

She stops at the door. "I can't believe you have had to come here like this, especially when the social worker has gone home for his safety. I will wait right here for you just in case. Please shout me if you need anything. I have never known foster carers to be sent here like this and put in this situation before. I thought social services usually took the children to the foster carers homes."

"Yes, I was led to believe that too." I say as I take a deep breath and enter the room, wondering what to expect.

Two young women are sitting on a large brown leather sofa on the right-hand side of the room, chatting quietly. They both appear to be in their late twenties. One is dressed in a grey suit, and the other has a long pencil skirt and a white blouse on, with black patterned tights. The one in a grey suit stands up. "Hi, I'm Emily from children's services. You must be the foster carer?"

"Yes, I'm Lacey," I reply, reaching out to return her handshake.

"This is Rose and Chase," Emily says.

Turning to the other end of the room, I see a young female holding a baby. She is wearing a scruffy-looking grey Lonsdale tracksuit. She must only be in her late teens to early twenties, around five feet tall, with long dark hair scraped back into a tight ponytail. She has a lip piercing and huge gold hooped earrings that balance on her shoulders.

"Hi, Rose, I'm Lacey," I say, unsure what else to say.

Rose shoots me a dirty look, but other than that, she seems quite calm; no tears. She doesn't seem either upset or angry, really. "I'm dying for a fag. I've been stuck here all day!" she moans.

I am stunned into silence. *Am I hearing right?*

Sensing the awkwardness, Emily steps in. "Lacey, why don't you tell Rose a little bit about your experience with children?"

I smile gratefully. "This is my first time fostering," I confess. "I used to work in nurseries whilst going to college to do my training in children and young people's workforce. I also have a little girl named Debbie, who has just started nursery school this year. She can't wait to meet Chase."

"Well, you better take care of him then." Rose says abruptly.

"Of course," I promise. And with that, she hands him over to me and, without a second glance, heads towards the door, pulling out a packet of twenty Richmond from her tracksuit bottoms pocket.

"Wow," I say, turning around to the social workers. "That wasn't what I expected."

19

The social workers exchange glances. "It's her third time," says the social worker in the pencil skirt who hasn't introduced herself. "She's got two other children from a previous relationship who were both taken separately into care and are now adopted together in the same family."

Emily hands over a changing bag and informs me that Chase is on four ounces of Cow & Gate milk every three hours.

I look down at Chase, who's wrapped up in his light-blue blanket with teddy bears, sleeping. He doesn't have much hair, just stray strands of light-brown hair starting to come through. He's sucking on thin air, and it hits me that I don't even know if he usually has a dummy. I get a quick glimpse of his brown eyes as he opens them and then closes them again as I settle him into the car seat. I ask a few more questions that I need answering before returning to my car and heading home.

It takes me twenty minutes to do the ten-minute drive home as there is a lot of traffic. It's quarter past four by the time I pull into the drive. As I unfasten the seat belt and lift Chase out of his seat, he opens his eyes again. "Hello, little man," I say. "I hope you have had a good sleep because there is a very excited little girl waiting to meet you." As soon as my keys turn in the door, I'm greeted by Debbie on the other side.

"Aww," she squeals in delight. "Can I hold him?"

"Let your mum get through the door first," my mum laughs.

After Debbie has changed out of her school uniform into her pink Me to You pyjamas and scraped her long light-golden brown hair back into a ponytail, I tell her to sit down on the sofa, and I gently place Chase into her arms. Chase looks up at her, and her bright blue eyes are locked on him.

"I'm going now," Mum says as she lifts her long black jacket from the coat peg. "I took Debbie for a McDonald's on the way back from school, so she's all sorted. I will get off and leave you three to settle now."

"Thank you, Mum," I say as she closes the front door behind her.

I check my phone to see no missed calls. I'm surprised that Robert still hasn't rang. Never mind, I think, tutting to myself. Chase starts to cry. He's probably due a feed. I place him down into the bouncer I have bought, and he screams even louder. "Sorry," I say. "Don't you like it in there? I need to put you down a minute if you want some milkies." As I lift him out, he stops screaming but continues to cry a little. I carry him into the kitchen and manage to make up his bottle with my left hand while holding him still in my right arm. I just need to cool it down. I realize that the jug is at the back of the bottom cupboard. I place him in his car seat, which I had left by the back door earlier when I arrived home. All of a sudden, he stops crying, snuggling his little head against the side of it.

By now, the milk has cooled to a nice lukewarm temperature. I gently lift Chase out of his car seat, and he starts to scream hysterically again, going bright red in the face until he eventually starts to suck his bottle, downing a full five ounces of milk that I had made just in case.

As the night goes on, I start to notice a pattern. Chase is constantly crying and only seems to stop when he is in his car seat. I can remember Robert saying he was left in a smoky room. I wonder if he was in the car seat?

At half past seven, I'm just about to take Debbie to bed when there is a loud, unexpected knock at the door. "Who is it, Mum?" Debbie asks, yawning. I open the door to see Robert.

"Oh, hiya," I say, surprised. "Come in." Robert walks into the living room, taking a seat on the black leather sofa furthest away, Debbie following him curiously behind.

"Isn't he cute?" Debbie says. "He cries a lot, though."

I laugh. "He only stops when he's in the car seat."

Robert gives me a sad look. "He was in his car seat most of the time in front of the TV when he was at home, so it may take him a while to settle."

*That explains it,* I think to myself. It's all scary and new to him here. The car seat is his comfort. The only place he feels safe. Robert apologizes for leaving me at court. "It wasn't meant to happen like that," he says. "His dad Raymond can be very intimidating, so I thought it was best that I left."

I can't help but think to myself, *Why didn't you ring? Why are you only coming around to explain now at half past seven at night? And if he's so intimidating to a grown man like yourself, then why is it okay for a twenty-four-year-old woman to have to walk into this situation with no ID badge and an empty car seat. It's lucky Raymond had already left and didn't spot me.*

Instead, I keep my thoughts to myself and let it slide.

"I still need my ID badge," I say, "and I'm still waiting on the setup money. I have had to run out this morning and grab what I can out of my pocket, but he still needs a lot more."

"Don't worry," he says, "I will sort it out."

An hour later, he's still chatting away. So far, I've heard all about the stresses of his caseloads and the difficulty he has had with Chase's parents. Debbie is standing by the window. She's pulled the curtains open slightly and is peering out at the dark winter rainfall. She turns to Robert. "Isn't it time for your bed?" she asks innocently. I'm cringing, but I can't help but release a giggle at the same time, which I quickly try to cover up with a fake cough.

It's eight thirty before Robert eventually leaves, and I finally settle Debbie to sleep, but I'm in for a long night with Chase.

# The contact centre

As I pull up in my car outside of the contact centre, I'm filled with dread. I see a young couple in their late teens come flying out of the front door, shouting. The boy turns to go back inside the centre, and the girl puts her hand on his shoulders, dragging him away. They walk to the bottom gates where they meet a crowd of about six or seven other boys and girls who appear to be waiting for them.

I sigh at the thought of getting out of the car and leaving my new red Clio parked here. Robert had explained to me that contacts would be twice a week on a Tuesday and a Thursday morning — ten o'clock until twelve o'clock. I was relieved that Debbie would be in school and would not have to come here with me. Although I'm glad that the contact supervisors would be supervising the contact, I still have the "joys" of dropping Chase off and talking to the parents and then seeing them again when going back into the room to collect him.

I still haven't met Raymond, and I hope that he has had time to calm down a little and isn't as aggressive towards me as he had been with the social workers. I look at the clock on my dashboard. It's five minutes to ten. I lift Chase from his car seat and pick up his changing bag, throwing it over my free shoulder.

The doors are locked, and I ring the bell. I'm greeted by an older woman in her mid-fifties. She's wearing smart black trousers and a grey blouse buttoned right up high to her neck. She gives me a stern look, then looks down at Chase, who is glancing around at his surroundings. "Have you got any ID?" the stern woman asks.

I explain that I'm new and that I am still waiting for my ID badge. After giving her my name, Chase's name and his date of birth, she seems satisfied and steps to one side, allowing us in. I step through and stand in reception, feeling awkward. I can hear loud voices coming from down the hall. "You're in room five," she says. I head down the hall. The walls are covered in numbers, cartoon characters, and the alphabet. A bit like a nursery, really.

I go past rooms one, two, three, and four and eventually get to room five set back at the end of the hall. I give a quick knock before entering. I recognize Chase's mum from the courtroom sat on her phone in the corner on a beanbag. I'm shocked to see a man at the side of her in his late forties. He's bald with grey bristles starting to appear and a week's worth of grey stubble. He's wearing jeans with tears down the sides and a dark blue hoodie.

His face is starting to wrinkle slightly with age. His eyes have bags underneath them, giving an impression of a hard life, years of drug abuse, no doubt. I assume this must be Raymond. "Hi, you must be Raymond?" I say.

Raymond just gives me a dirty look and goes straight to Chase. "Come here, my son," he booms in a loud tone as if making a point with the "my".

I smile and step back. He lifts Chase in the air and stumbles backwards as he does. Just then, a woman in her thirties enters the room carrying her laptop.

"He's due a feed in about an hour," I say. "And his nappy was done half an hour ago, so it should be okay for a little while."

Raymond is now making loud noises, blowing raspberries to Chase. Rose is still not looking up from her Blackberry phone. I then notice her small black earphones connected from her phone to her ears. With that, I gently close the door behind me and leave.

By the time I get home, I realize I have only got an hour before I need to set back out to collect Chase. I dial Robert's number, and it goes straight through to voicemail. I then ring Marie, whose phone also goes straight to voicemail. I leave a quick message reminding her that I need my ID badge sorting out and that I still haven't received the startup grant. I ask her to call me back ASAP and put the phone down.

Marie is my supervising social worker. She's the one who should be sorting all this really, but I haven't heard from her in a while. I make a quick ham and cheese sandwich and a cup of coffee before heading back out to collect Chase. The same woman answers the door and lets me straight in this time. "You know where you are going," she says. It's more of a statement than a question.

I knock on door number five. "Come in," a woman's voice says. It sounds like the contact supervisor.

"Why has my son got fluff on him?" Raymond shouts.

I'm taken aback. "It will just be off his blanket," I reply calmly.

"His nappy was soaked too!"

"Well, I am sorry about that. It was changed right before I left the house to bring him here," I say, trying not to let my frustration show. I glance at the contact supervisor who is hiding behind her laptop, not giving any attention to the situation in front of her. *Thanks a bunch*, I think to myself.

I lean down to the floor to greet Chase. Rose quickly gets in front of me, scooping him up. She starts to put on his coat but seems to be struggling.

"What you doing, stupid?" Raymond shouts, making Chase jump. Me too, for that matter. Raymond snatches Chase from Rose and pulls his arms through his coat rather roughly. "There," he shouts, stepping closer to Rose's face and pulling on her arm. Rose says nothing and drops her head down, walking behind Raymond. I can't help but feel sorry for her. She appears like just a lost little girl under his clutches, obeying his orders.

As we leave, I glance back at the contact supervisor, hoping she's writing all of this down. She's now packing up her laptop. As I walk to the car, Raymond follows me. He's still got Chase. I open my car door, and he pushes past me, fastening him in his seat. He then takes what seems to be forever to say his goodbyes. Surely, they shouldn't be coming to my car like this? I thought a contact supervisor would have walked out with us, given the fact they know the risks.

I ask myself if I have made a mistake fostering. This is far from the job I thought it would be.

# Six months later

I wake to the sun shining brightly through the gap in the curtains. Chase is giggling in his cot at the side of my bed. He turns straight to me, staring at me with his big brown eyes and smiles.

"Good morning, little man." I smile back. It's been six months now since he came to me, and I'm trying my very best not to fall in love with him, but it's proving to be difficult. In the past six months, I have not seen the social workers as often as I am supposed to. The guidelines say that they should be coming out every six weeks to check on Chase, but they rarely do. We have gone up to twelve weeks with no communication. I have accepted now that I won't be seeing any sign of my ID badge, but I did eventually receive the start-up grant.

Contacts have become a part of my weekly routine now. Chase's dad's aggression has calmed down a little with me, although it is a regular occurrence with Rose, constantly snapping at her. A few months back, I had turned up to one contact to find Rose stood outside the gates, waiting for me alone. I was surprised to hear that Raymond had been sentenced to six weeks in prison for a fight that he had in their flat while Chase was present and still in their care.

I couldn't help but shudder at the thought of what else this poor baby had been through in the first eight weeks of his life before coming to me. Rose seemed more confident, happy, and outgoing while he wasn't around. That quickly came to an abrupt stop six weeks later when Raymond turned up shouting at her for spending money while he had been away.

I had also found myself in some vulnerable situations over the months where I had to attend regular check-up appointments for Chase and meet Raymond and Rose there as they always insisted on coming, and the social worker was never available, so it was all on me. To my amazement, Chase is such a calm, content baby, easily pleased, and has already been sleeping through the night, which is just as well considering all the daily paperwork and late-night training groups I'm having to juggle around him.

For such a full-time job, around the clock with no breaks, I cannot believe that I only get a ninety-pound-a-week wage. Once Chase has either returned to his parents or been adopted, I am going to hand my notice in and look for social worker assistant jobs. They seem to have a laid-back job with a lot better pay. At least they switch off at the end of the day. My heart sinks again at the thought of handing Chase over.

I scoop Chase from his cot now and give him a big cuddle before getting dressed and ready for a day out in town. We are meeting my friend Emma who I rarely see these days. The schools are closed for a week, and

Debbie has gone to see her dad for the day. I was almost nineteen when I had Debbie, and her dad was almost twenty-one. We stayed together until Debbie turned one, but then the relationship broke down, and we both went our separate ways, wanting different things in life.

Debbie is not due home until five, giving me the full day out with Chase. When I arrive in town, I make my way to a little pub with a suitable family area. "Wow, he's grown." Emma beams as she walks over to us. We order two Cokes from the waitress and begin chatting.

"I can't believe social services have hardly been in touch," Emma says.

"I know. We are getting used to the answerphone now." I laugh.

Chase is lying in his pushchair with his favourite soft blue blanket. He's making his usual croaking noises like he's struggling to breathe. He's been doing this since he came to me. I have been concerned about him foaming at the mouth too, but I've been told it's nothing to worry about and that he will grow out of it. I pick up the menu and start scanning through the mains when Emma screams, "Lacey!"

I look up to see Chase, who is sitting in his pushchair. The wheezing has stopped now. No croaking noises. He's gone slightly blue, and I can't hear him breathing.

Panic hits me. "Chase!" I scream. I stand up and step towards him, start unbuckling his straps, and quickly scoop him up. Just then, he lets out a breath, but it's still very weak, and the wheezing seems worse than usual. He's gone a more noticeable shade of blue. I say my goodbyes and head back to the multistorey where I've parked my car. Social services had laughed at me when I had mentioned he was foaming at the mouth, accusing me of being dramatic. My concerns had been right. I knew something was wrong.

I drive to the nearest walk-in centre, checking the reflection in my mirror throughout the drive to keep an eye on Chase. I'm seen almost straight away. I carry Chase in my arms and take a seat across from the doctor. He tells me his name, but I'm staring at Chase, trying to keep my arms steady from shaking, so I don't quite catch what he's saying.

I quickly explain what has happened. The doctor takes Chase from me and places him on the bed. He is listening for his heartbeat and using different equipment. I'm glued to the spot, shaking. *I better ring social services,* I think. There should be a number saved in my phone for the emergency team. *Did I ever get given the number?*

I hear the word "ambulance". I am struggling to take it all in. The doctor is explaining something about "sats".

"They are low. He will need to go to the main hospital."

It feels like a lifetime later, but it must only be several minutes until I'm in an ambulance with him. He's lying on a little bed in the ambulance, and I'm perched at his side, holding his little hand. He's got an oxygen mask on that looks far too big for his little face. He looks so vulnerable. I wipe away a stray tear that's fallen down my cheek.

After ten minutes, we arrive at the hospital. The nurses rush over to us, and Chase is taken to a ward and given a little cot bed. *Please be okay,* I silently pray, and then it hits me. "I love you," I whisper as I stroke his face.

# The hospital

"His name is Chase!" I scream down the phone, unable to keep calm. Chase has been in the hospital for two nights now. I found the emergency out-of-hours number for the local authority on Google. How did we manage before Google was invented? When explaining that Chase had stopped breathing and was taken to hospital by ambulance, I don't know what I expected. A social worker to turn up to the hospital? His parents turn up, escorted by a social worker, maybe? Nothing could have prepared me for the response I got. Instead, they just agreed to log the information on the system, said they would not need to inform the parents, and thanked me for the information, asking me to keep them updated.

So now here I am ringing to give an update, but the young-sounding man on the phone can't seem to find Chase on his system. "I'm sorry, I have not long arrived on my shift. I can't find anything about a Chase in hospital," he says now.

After explaining what has happened once again, he logs it all on the computer. I don't bother to thank him and put down the phone.

I return to the sensory play area where my mum and Debbie are playing with Chase, pointing out his reflection in the mirror. Chase is touching his face reflection curiously, smiling. "The doctor has checked him over," Mum says. "He's free to go, just waiting for the discharge form."

After a day and a half on oxygen, Chase was starting to breathe a lot better, and the wheezing had improved. They had kept him in another night without the oxygen and are now pleased to discharge him. The doctor had said it was bronchitis. Thirty minutes later, a nurse returns with a piece of paper saying "Discharge slip" at the top of it. I thank her and all of the other staff for their help, and we all make our way to Mum's car. I'm so tired. I haven't slept in days and have barely eaten.

I can't help but wonder what has been said to the parents. Surely, they must have told them? Are they angry at not being told immediately? I know I would be. As soon as I arrive home, Mum watches the kids, and I jump straight into bed, feeling immediate relief. I'm filled with dread at what's to come at the next contact. Will I have to be the one to tell Raymond and Rose? Will they take their anger out on me? Tiredness swoops in on me, and before I know it, I'm fast asleep.

# The aftermath

It's been an emotional weekend, and I've had barely a few hours' sleep. I feel like I need to hear Chase breathing, and I can't stop going over the phone calls with the emergency team and stressing about seeing Chase's mum and dad.

On top of this, I'm trying not to think about Chase's future. Will he go back to Rose and Raymond? I just can't imagine the life he will have with them. Or will he go for adoption? I shudder as an image of me saying goodbye pops up in my head. How can I watch him leave, knowing I will never see him again?

I try to rub the image from my mind when I hear a knock at the door. Peeking through the spyhole, I see Chase's latest social worker. She taps again. I open the front door with Chase in my arms and invite her in. "Hi, what are you doing here? We weren't expecting you."

"I got the message this morning," Jill says now. "Is he okay?"

I tell Jill what happened, and she quickly scribbles it all down in her notebook, stopping only to ask questions. When she's finished, she jumps up and starts to gather her paperwork together.

Before I can stop myself, the anger comes out. "Where on earth was the emergency team?" I blurt out at her. "Have you told Chase's parents?"

She stops still by the door and turns back to face me. "The social worker on the phone to you got his paperwork muddled up with another child. The other parents are not allowed to see their child because of some serious issues. We are going to ring Raymond and Rose to explain and apologize. They may want to make a complaint."

"Well," I say, "I'm just about to head for the contact centre. They have contact in thirty minutes."

Jill rushes off, and I quickly race around, getting ready for his contact. I pull up outside the contact centre just in time, finding Rose and Raymond standing by the front door waiting for my arrival.

"Why the hell did we not get told?" Raymond shouts across the car park. He's red in the face with anger and making his way towards me. I get Chase out of the car and keep walking to the front doors, making them turn back. I quickly knock on the door whilst telling Raymond calmly that I'm sorry they weren't told, but I had informed social services, and they made that decision. The contact supervisor opens the door, and we walk down into the room.

"He's my fucking son." Raymond is shouting now. I apologize again and leave the room. As I let myself out at the front of the building, I can still hear Raymond shouting. He's so intimidating. Poor Chase must be scared. Gosh, when I signed up to be a foster carer, I never would have dreamt it could be so awful. The social workers certainly don't tell you that you will be dealing with the fallout from their mistakes and left with no support like this.

I have two hours before I need to pick Chase back up. I pray that Raymond has calmed down by then, although I can hardly blame him. I can't imagine how I would feel if my child had stopped breathing and spent all weekend in the hospital, and I didn't get told.

I sit in a local cafe sipping hot chocolate before it's time to make my way back to the centre. As I knock on the door, I can hear Raymond raising his voice. He doesn't sound happy. So much for hoping he would have calmed down by now. I slowly open the door and step into the room cautiously.

Chase is lying under a blue play gym with dangling fish. He turns his head towards me and lets out an excited squeal, smiling at me. "He had a piece of fluff on him again," Raymond says. "You need to be careful; he could have swallowed it."

I'm taken aback. I remember a conversation in training about how parents can pick on the foster carer's parenting as a way of holding onto control and feeling anger towards the one who is doing the job they failed. It makes sense, I suppose, but surely a bit of fluff is a bit extreme. Especially as this is the second time that he has complained about it when it has come from the blanket that they got him.

"Oh, I'm sorry," I say, now looking at Raymond. "It must have come from his blanket."

Raymond glares at me for what seems like ages until I break eye contact. Feeling awkward, I go over to Chase to say hello. Chase responds with another smile and puts his arms out for me in a gesture for me to pick him up. Raymond quickly steps in and starts to put Chase's shoes on. "Move," he shouts to Rose. Rose gets off the far sofa and starts walking over, gathering Chase's belongings.

Not for the first time, I wonder if the contact supervisor has noted any of this. This time it's a male in his early thirties. He's sat on a chair in the far corner looking at his laptop but doesn't seem to be typing. As we leave, Raymond is at the side of me, and Rose is trailing behind with her phone speaker blasting a familiar Eminem song. Raymond puts Chase into the car, forgetting to put the car seat strap around, and we say our goodbyes.

As I drive off, I see Raymond making his way up the street, with Rose following several steps behind. She's staring down at her phone in a world of her own. I make my way home.

# A life-changing decision

"Debbie," I shout up the stairs for the fourth time. "You are going to be late for school." Debbie strolls casually down the stairs, and I hand her school bag to her. It's a dull, wet, cloudy day outside. We put our hoods up and run to the car. I fit Chase's car seat in the car whilst Debbie climbs into her fitted booster seat, and we head off for school.

After dropping Debbie off at school, I drop Chase off with my sister Lauren. Lucky enough, it's her day off work today, or I would be stuck. All babysitters must be police checked. I had chosen my mum, dad, and Lauren.

My dad works nights as a machine operator, Mum works as a dinner lady in my old school, and Lauren works in a clothes shop. Lauren is five years younger than me and still lives at home with our mum and dad. I think most of the training and meetings are in the day so that it's easier for foster carers with school-age children, but for me, with a baby, it's proving difficult in the daytime. I thank Lauren and hand over the changing bag, giving Chase a big kiss as I leave.

I'm a little late by the time I arrive at the event. It's a quarterly catch-up where all the foster carers meet up at the local cricket club and listen to all the latest news and announcements. I grab a glass of water and scan the room for a seat. Sue waves over at me from the far corner. I walk across and take a seat next to hers. "How are things going?" I ask.

"Not too good, really," she replies.

I met Sue at several previous training courses. Sue is a tall, slim woman in her late forties with shoulder-length brown hair. She has grown-up children and started foster caring babies a year ago, like me. Sue still has her first placement with her, a one-year-old girl who was placed with her at just two weeks old as a result neglect. She's had many issues with her social worker not turning up.

The last time we spoke, she was in a panic. A week before her holiday, that had been booked six months before, and the social worker had not got the baby's passport after months of being asked.

"What is it?" I say now. "You didn't miss your holiday, did you?"

"No," she replies. "We had a lovely time in Spain. Jean loved it. We got the passport eventually, days before."

"Then what's the matter?" I ask.

Sue then begins to tell me that Jean has gone up for adoption. My heart sinks at the thought of Chase going for adoption. I've had him for ten months now, a lot longer than expected.

I'm shocked into silence as Sue tells me what's been going on. Jean's social worker isn't sure who

Jean's birth father is. Her birth mother had many one-night stands, a few with Asian men. In the adoption files, the social worker has said that the baby is white, as she will get adopted out easier that way. Jean has brown eyes and dark hair. It's hard to tell if she is mixed race.

At the end of the two-hour talk, I say my goodbyes to Sue and tell her to stay in touch. As I drive home, I can't stop thinking about what I've just learnt. Are there any limits to what they do? How can they do this and get away with it? I've known for some time about the complacency of social services, but this is such a deliberate act. It makes it so much worse.

All day I can't stop thinking about Chase's future. At nine o'clock, both kids are fast asleep in bed, and I'm lying on the sofa. The soaps have just finished, and I have completed my daily diary write-up. I pick up the phone and ring my mum. I've made a big decision, and I need to get it off my chest. Mum picks up on the first ring.

"Hiya," I say nervously.

"Everything okay?" Mum asks.

"I erm… I have something to tell you."

"What is it, sweetheart?"

I just blurt it out. "If Chase goes for adoption, I'm going to put in a request to adopt him myself."

The phone line goes quiet for what feels like forever. I hold my breath and wait.

"I knew you shouldn't have become a foster carer," Mum says now. "This was meant to be a job. You can't just throw your career away." Mum sounds upset.

"I'm adopting him, Mum. I love him. I'm all he has. Social services have done nothing but fail him. It's up to you if you support me or not, but you won't change my mind." I put the phone down and burst into tears.

Five minutes later, my phone rings. It's Mum. I pause and contemplate hanging up. I decide against it and pick up but don't speak. Instead, I wait.

"Hiya, sweetheart," Mum says in a weak voice. She sounds choked up like she's been crying. "I've been thinking, and you are right. Chase is part of our family now. I will support you all the way."

I then break down again, crying, but this time they are tears of happiness. The decision is made. He's staying. I can't wait to tell Debbie. I know that I went into fostering as a job, but he's settled here. I will eventually find a better job.

# One month later

It's been a mad month. Chase's social worker came around a few weeks ago and told me that she had someone in mind whom she would like to adopt Chase. I couldn't believe what I was hearing. It was a week before the court hearing, so the judge had not yet granted an adoption order. Surely, she should not already be looking for adopters? Besides, the adopted parents of Chase's older siblings would need to be asked first. It's always best to keep siblings together.

After failed drug tests, the judge did agree that Chase would not return home to his parents. The social worker informed me that the adopters of Chase's siblings had said they didn't wish to pursue adopting Chase. I then type out an email to the head of adoption, letting them know that I wish to apply to adopt Chase. The reply was very brief, arranging to come around to my house to discuss it further.

So here I sit, waiting for the doorbell to ring. I'm so nervous. This time in an hour, I'll either be celebrating the prospect of adopting Chase and giving him the life, he deserves, looking forward to his birthdays, Christmas's, watching him grow, or I will be facing handing him over to strangers, knowing that I will never see him again.

"Pack it in, Lacey," I say aloud to myself, rubbing away a stray tear escaping down my cheek. I've had Chase since he was just eight weeks old. We are all he knows. Surely, they will be happy for him to remain here?

I'm a qualified child practitioner, and I've been employed by them as a local authority foster carer. They have no possible reason to say that I am not suitable or that this isn't the best place for Chase. I've got this. The doorbell goes. Chase looks up from his play gym where he's lying. I try to steady my shaking hand as I open the door.

The social worker is a stern-looking older lady in her late fifties. She has short bleach blonde hair and is wearing a skirt and blouse with a long grey blazer. She is wearing an ID badge on a long chain around her neck with her photograph.

In her right hand, she holds a black ring binder folder. 'I'm Audrey,' she says sternly.

"Yes, come in." I smile, show Audrey to the living room, and offer her a seat. Audrey sits down and glances at Chase. 'And this is Chase," I say as I lift him onto the sofa with me.

Audrey replies with a quick hello. "Right, shall we start?" she says, opening her file. "I brought your assessment information with me from your fostering files."

I can see a load of writing with parts she must have gone through and highlighted in red.

"So why do you want to adopt him?"

"I have had him nearly a year now," I reply. "Chase is a lovely boy, and he's very settled here with us. He is close to my family, and my daughter Debbie adores him. I love him like my own."

"Well, he isn't your own, is he?"

"I don't pretend he is," I reply angrily. "I respect that he has a mum and a dad, and I would never take their place, but that doesn't mean that I don't have a strong bond with him."

"We will not be processing your application for adoption," Audrey says now.

My heart sinks, and my throat tightens. I can feel tears starting to come. I fight to keep them back and keep my voice steady as I speak. "I don't understand. He's been here so long and is happy. Why move him like that?"

"Fostering and adoption are two very different things," she replies like I'm stupid. "Your job is to foster, not to adopt. I've also noticed that you haven't completely ruled out having another child in the future, which would make Chase a middle child."

Just then, Debbie runs in with a cereal bar half-opened.

"I hope that's not your breakfast." Audrey sniggers before standing up and picking up her folder. Debbie stares at her, then goes over to Chase and squeezes up next to him on the sofa, stroking his face. "I'm sorry it wasn't better news," Audrey says as she walks towards the door. I manage a weak goodbye and close the door before bursting into tears.

# The beginning of a long fight

I haven't slept a wink all night, just tossing and turning. I can't stop staring at Chase. He's peacefully sleeping without a care in the world. I'm going to have to say goodbye to him and pack his little things, hand him over to adopters. Life will be so strange without him. One thing's for sure, I won't be foster caring again. I knew it would be hard, but it's been so much longer than I was told it would be.

Chase is still not sitting up or crawling yet. I can't help but worry about him. I hope his new mummy and daddy will love him as much as I do and give him the life he deserves. A part of me wants him to hurry up and go. I can't handle the pain much longer, waiting to lose him.

Debbie comes running into my room. "Is he awake, Mummy? I've made him a picture." She leans over his cot with a drawing. "That's me, you, and look, there's you, baby Chase, by me."

Tears stream down my face. "What's the matter, Mummy?" Debbie climbs into bed and cuddles up next to me.

"The thing is, Debbie, Chase will be going soon to his new family."

"No." She sobs. "Why?"

"Well, we are only looking after him, aren't we? Like we talked about, do you remember?"

"But why can't we keep him? You can look after him, Mum. I will help, I promise." Debbie starts to sob uncontrollably.

"Shh, it's okay," I soothe.

The sun is starting to stream through the curtains; Chase begins to stir. After getting both kids dressed and giving them breakfast, I settle them in the living room with *CBeebies* and sneak out of the room. I have to fight. I will not give up. I start to google a list of local solicitors and write down their numbers.

I take a deep breath and ring the first on the list. "Hi," I say when they answer. "I'm a local authority foster carer, and I would like to apply to adopt my foster son through the courts as social services are declining my adoption request."

"Oh," she replies. There is a long silence. "I'm sorry, this is not something we can take on."

"Oh right," I reply. "Thank you anyway." I then hang up and dial the second number.

I repeat myself.

"Sorry, I'm not sure taking on the local authority is something we do," he says.

I say my goodbyes and hang up. Three phone calls later, and I'm getting similar responses. "What is going on? There must be someone who has the guts to take on a case against the local authority, surely?" I shout out loud.

I go back to my Google search and find several more solicitor firms, then look for several more, further afield just in case. I start again. I'm not giving up. Someone must be out there that can help. Three hours later, I've got through a total of fifteen solicitors, all saying anything from, "Sorry, we don't deal with that area," to "This is quite a complex case, not something we have dealt with before." Feeling defeated, I make a cup of tea then ring my friend Marie. Marie picks up on the first ring. "Hiya, Lacey, I was about to ring you. How are things?"

I tell Marie everything, barely stopping for breath.

"It's ridiculous," Marie says. "He's happy with you. I don't understand the reason you can't just adopt him. Everywhere I go, I see signs crying out for adopters."

I've known Marie since we were young. We grew up together. She lived with her mum just down the street from where I lived with my mum, dad, and sister.

Marie's mum has autism and raised Marie alone after her dad passed away. It's not until I grew up that I realized how tough it must have been for them and what a strong person her mum was.

"Try my solicitor," Marie says now. "She was really good." Marie had split from her partner last year and had gone to court over her two boys Paul and John.

I thank Marie and take the number but know that I have no chance in hell of her taking on this case when so many big firms won't. I arrange to meet up with Marie at the weekend with the boys, Debbie and Chase. We haven't met up in a while. I promise to text her later and hang up. I text my mum the number asking her to remind me to ring this number tomorrow. I suddenly have an idea. I don't need a solicitor. I could fill the court forms out and take on the local authority myself. I add court forms to my list, then Citizens' Advice, family rights, and a few others. I then add MP to the list. Maybe he can help. I will find his email address and write to him tonight when the kids are in bed.

Satisfied I still have options and hope, I go into the living room and play with the kids. I've done enough for one day. Tomorrow is a new day.

# The parents' wishes

I have a busy day ahead. I'm waiting in town with Chase to meet his parents. I sometimes offer to do this when the contact centre is unavailable or if we have had a doctor's appointment, causing us to miss the contact centre. I have had no direct aggressive behaviour from his mum or dad in a while, just the odd complaint at contact. The aggression seems to be aimed at social workers mainly. When I get home, I have a lot more phone calls and emails to chase up, so I'm grateful for the break.

Raymond and Rose come strolling around the corner. Rose is following behind Raymond. "Hello," Raymond says. Rose smiles and leans over to greet Chase in his pram. "I'm fucking fuming," Raymond says, raising his voice.

I'm taken aback. *What now?* I think to myself.

"What's the matter?" I say, hoping it's not another issue over Chase. I've got into the habit of giving Chase a check over before contact. This is where I check his nails are cut and clean, his nose is clean, and there is no fluff on him before leaving the house.

"That daft bitch of a social worker has got Chase up for adoption. She has said my mum and sister can't have him because my mum's too old. I've seen social workers ready to pop their clogs. She's taking the piss. Our son is not going for adoption, or they will know about it!"

"I can see why you're upset," I say, "but can you please try not to get angry and swear in front of Chase."

"Well, why can't you adopt him?" Raymond says now.

I'm stunned into silence. After all the grief they give me, and they want me to adopt him?

"He's happy with you," Raymond says now.

I find myself being honest. It feels like a relief to let it all out. "Well, actually," I say, "I'm very fond of Chase and would love to give him a permanent home. I will be sad to see him go. I have tried to adopt him myself, but I have been turned down too."

"Bullshit," Raymond says.

"Calm down, Raymond, and watch your language," I remind him.

"You don't want him at all," he says. "They would not turn you down. You're the foster carer. They employed you. You passed all their checks."

"Actually, they have," I reply. "They have said that I can't have him in case I have another child in the future."

"You've got to be kidding me," Raymond says, stunned.

I look at Rose, who is standing over Chase with her head down. "It's like they just want to adopt him out," she says.

I don't mention that the social worker has had someone in mind the whole time. I change the subject, asking them where they fancy going. They choose a local park, a ten-minute walk away, and we start to head off up the road when a group of people approach.

"This your chap?" a scruffy-looking girl in a hoodie asks.

"Yeah, this is Chase," Rose says. "This is his foster carer."

The girl scowls at me, and the rest of the group look over. "They took my four too," she says now.

"Child snatchers," the lad next to her says, putting his arm around her neck.

One of the four other lads stood behind asks, "You got a spare fifty pence?"

"No," Rose replies.

The lad looks at Chase's basket and sees a pack of Fruit Shoot. "Can I pinch one of them, man?"

Rose looks towards me, and the rest of the group turn their heads to me. I nod at Rose. When she's given him a Fruit Shoot, I say, "Come on, we need to head off."

They say their goodbyes, and carry on walking. *I hope I don't see them again*, I think to myself, knowing that I could bump into them up here when I'm shopping with Debbie and that they will recognize Chase and me.

Chase plays on the swings when we arrive at the park. Both parents take turns pushing him. Apart from a conversation about a fight they had last week, which involved the police, the contact goes well. They walk with me to my car, which is parked in the multistorey car park, and with some prompting, fasten Chase into his car seat.

"Keep fighting for our son," Raymond says. I assure him that I will do all I can for Chase and leave, heading for home where Debbie and my mum are waiting for us.

As I arrive through the door carrying Chase in my arms, my mum comes rushing to me. "I've rung that number you sent me," she says. "The solicitor was lovely, and she is going to represent you in court. She says that your best fight would be to obtain a special guardianship order known as an SGO for Chase."

"What?" I say, unable to contain my excitement. "What's that?"

"It's a court order that gives you overriding parental responsibility. It means that Chase gets to stay with you forever, but unlike adoption, you will have to give contact still to parents. It might be six times a year. You can't change his surname or leave the country for more than a certain amount of time, but apart from that, you make all decisions to care for him. You get to keep him." Mum smiles.

I struggle to get my words out for a few minutes. Relief, happiness, and excitement flood through me all at once, but I'm scared to get my hopes up. It doesn't feel real somehow, and there's still a chance we could lose the case. The local authority is bound to have a good solicitor and fight for adoption.

"That's amazing," I say to Mum. "I can't believe you rang them and sorted it."

"You know what I'm like." She laughs. "Now give him here." She reaches out for Chase, who stares at her. He gurgles and smiles in her arms.

# The court hearing

I sit, nervously waiting, gathered around a table with my
mum, Raymond, and Rose. The social workers sit across
from us, drinking coffee, talking amongst themselves.

"We just want to give Chase a good life and will
support any contact the judge agrees to," my mum says
now.

"Hopefully, they will agree," Raymond says.

Today is the first time my mum has met Raymond
and Rose. I don't think she was expecting this, despite
my warnings. I try not to laugh as she engages in a
conversation with Raymond.

"She's been messaging another man," Raymond
shouts. A few people sitting behind us turn around. I
cringe. "How would you feel if your husband was on
Facebook talking to other women?" he asks.

My mum pauses: she looks stuck for words. "That's
not good, is it?" she replies, then turns to me. I give her
a look, still trying not to laugh. How uncomfortable must
she feel? I hear our names being called and see the relief
flush across Mum's face. Mum lets out a sigh of relief
as we all get up and head to the courtroom. I take a seat
behind my solicitor, who introduces herself as Amy
Field. Both parents sit behind their solicitors. They have

one each. Raymond has a male in his late thirties representing him, and Rose has a female solicitor, also in her late thirties, representing her. Chase's social worker sits at the back with her head down. The local authority solicitor is at the side of the room next to the woman who has previously introduced herself as Chase's guardian. She is sitting next to a large bloke in his late twenties wearing a grey suit and whom I can only presume is representing her.

"All rise!" says the judge at the front. We all stand up.

"Stand up," Raymond shouts. I look over and see Rose sitting down in a world of her own. She then looks at everyone standing up and quickly joins us. I keep a straight face and look straight ahead at the judge, ignoring the glares from Chase's social worker. I cross my fingers and pray a silent prayer for Chase.

The local authority does not dispute the guardianship, much to my amazement.

They have realized that they don't have a leg to stand on, but they are requesting that they do a special guardianship assessment on me to see if I'm suitable to take on a special guardianship order case. Panic rises through me. No wonder they aren't disputing the SGO. They will just find something to fail me on during the SGO assessment.

My solicitor stands up. She raises concerns that the social worker has adopted parents in mind before the court order has even been made and that she has an agenda to adopt Chase out, so she can't be trusted to do a fair assessment on me. I hold my breath. The judge agrees that a private assessment should be done on me by an independent social worker and that the fees are to be paid by the local authority. I breathe out a sigh of relief. It's hardly like I could afford to pay for it with my ninety-pound wage.

As we leave the courtroom, the social worker barges past me, tutting. I thank Amy for her help and ask her what will happen next. Amy explains that an independent social worker will be out to assess me, and then the court order should be granted so I won't need her again.

"What if they don't agree?" I ask.

"Try not to worry," Amy says. "The SGO assessment is the same as your fostering assessment. She won't try to make you fail. She will have an open mind." I thank her and go over to my mum, who is waiting patiently by the coffee machine.

"Well?" Mum says as we leave the court and make our way to the car park. I begin to tell Mum what's happened in court.

We arrive at my house, where the kids are waiting with Lauren. Lauren is pleased to hear the news. "Let's go out for tea," she says. We collect Chase's things and get ready to go out.

"We have some celebrating to do," I say, skipping to collect Chase's coat. I feel so relieved, but I can't help but feel a little bit nervous too. I won't rest properly until the court order is stamped and social services are out of my life. Amy mentioned that they would have to pay me an allowance for Chase, but I daren't fight them too much for that. I will just have to get a part-time job.

# The private assessment

I pace back across the living room, looking out of the front window. The independent social worker, Jeanette is ten minutes late. She was due to come at ten o'clock. My heart is racing so fast. I sit back down again and lift Chase onto my knee. His life, all our lives, depend on today. I can't mess this up. I need to stay calm, I remind myself, for the tenth time this morning. The doorbell rings, and I jump up, racing towards the front door, placing Chase in his bouncer. I take a deep breath before pulling open the door. Jeanette is in her mid-fifties with shoulder-length blonde hair.

She's dressed in a smart skirt, tights, and white blouse with a loose pink cardy adding a casual touch. She reaches out her hand to introduce herself as the independent social worker, and I immediately relax in her friendly presence. I make Jeanette a cup of tea. When I return to the living room, I find her crouched down on the floor at Chase's level, talking to him in a soothing babyish voice, asking him what his toys are. I smile, and Jeanette smiles warmly back at me.

"I can see why you have fallen in love." She laughs. "He's adorable." Jeanette asks about Chase and makes friendly conversation. I tell her about everything that's been going on with the local authority social workers. She doesn't seem surprised.

"Unfortunately, I see a lot worse all the time," she confides. "You would not believe how many times I have assessed families who are on the verge of losing their children because of a social worker with a grudge."

I've never thought of it like that before. I've always thought that if a parent loses their child, then there must be evidence, but now, seeing how much social workers can twist things, it doesn't surprise me that there are some cases out there where this has happened. I shudder at the thought of them trying to build a case that isn't there to remove Debbie. Words can't explain how their parents must have felt.

After a few hours of going through the paperwork, Jeanette tells me that she's got most of what she needs. The assessments are very similar to the fostering assessment, so she has used a lot of that paperwork for the details she needs. At last, I feel positive and very lucky to have such a friendly, down-to-earth social worker. I think that is what it is all about, really, like playing the lottery. If you get a bad social worker, then your chances of winning are slim to none.

I ask Jeanette what made her go into independent work. Jeanette tells me some brief stories. One about a set of parents who were schoolteachers, mixed race, and didn't speak much English. She tells me how the local authority social worker was trying to remove their children, but she found no concerns and helped them to keep their children. It's heart-breaking, and whilst I'm feeling more positive about my case, I feel like the system is a lot worse than I ever believed it to be. How worried must their parents and children have felt? It's a scary thought.

Jeanette also explains to me that it works both ways. She has investigated cases where children should have been removed, and the local authority had failed to act. There have been some really disturbing abuse cases that social services have allowed to go on. I don't think I could do Jeanette's job, but I'm glad she does it. It's nice to see a social worker who is fair and investigates things the way that they should be investigated. She must have helped a lot of families and saved a lot of children.

Jeanette pauses and looks at me now. She must have sensed my fear despite my best efforts to keep a straight face. "Don't worry," she says now. "I can see how much you love him. You have a lovely environment for him and have had him for a long time. This is the best option for him. My report will be positive. It's then just down to the judge to agree on a special guardianship order." She starts to place all her reports back into her large open bag. "It was lovely to meet you," she says, and I let her out, thanking her.

Somehow, I don't think I could ever thank her enough. I could have very easily ended up with a social worker no better than the local authority ones. I shudder at the thought as I close the door, turning back to the living room.

I ring my mum and tell her how well it has gone. She too breathes a sigh of relief. "She said it should just all go through, that she can't find any reason why I would not be suitable to care for Chase long term."

"That's brilliant," Mum says. "Now try to relax and concentrate on Christmas. Enjoy the kids."

That is exactly what I do until 19 December, when I receive a phone call to tell me that the courts are granting the guardianship order. I burst into tears, but this time, tears of joy. No more worry. This little boy is staying with us forever. I could not have wished for a better Christmas present. I rush out to get some food and balloons. We are going to throw a party to celebrate. It's finally all over.

Little did I realize at this time that this was just the beginning. There would be more to come. Much, much more.

# Two years on

"Mum, come quick, you need to see this."

I run up the stairs. Debbie's bedroom door swings open. Debbie gives me a smirk. "I told you." Chase stands at the window, banging his head on the glass, making handprints with the chocolate he must have sneaked from out of the cupboard. The toybox is thrown on its side. Toys are sprawled everywhere. I can barely make out the colour of the carpet. There are that many toys. I tiptoe across to the window where Chase is jumping up and down, squealing.

"Chase, down." He stares out into the back garden.

"Playhouse there."

"Chase, come down," I repeat, raising my voice slightly.

I reach out to lift him down when he suddenly kicks out, grabs two large chunks of my hair, one each side, and throws himself at me. I try to prise his hands, but they have a firm grip. His squealing is getting louder. He lets go and drops to the floor, rolling around kicking the wall. "Here we go again." Debbie tuts.

So much has happened in just a few years. I could cry thinking about the calm baby he once was. I waited so long for him to walk. It felt like it would never happen, and then, at the age of almost two, with the help of a physiotherapist, he went from not being able to walk to running everywhere.

With the help of speech therapy, he eventually learned to talk a little. He says the same few words constantly yet doesn't respond to what we say to him. It's like he can't see or hear that we are here. I may as well be invisible. I have started saying his name and one direct word to get his attention, but this rarely works either.

Chase spins his head in circles; his eyes roll back. The light switch catches his eyes. He pushes the switch down, then up, down, then up. The lights flicker on and off. *Here we go*, I think to myself. "Chase, time for nursery." Chase carries on flicking the light switch.

"Chase! I have got your train," Debbie says now, waving a blue train at Chase to distract him. I smile at Debbie. I'm so proud of her. She's amazing with him. You would never think she was only seven.

Chase carries on flicking the light, oblivious to her presence. I stoop down to Chase's level. "Chase, car." I place my arm around his shoulder and pull him towards me. Chase lets out an almighty squeal, drops to the floor, and crawls under the bed, clinging to the wooden panels underneath.

"I can't be late, not again," Debbie says.

"Go get in the car, Debbie."

I reach under the bed and try to pull Chase out. By the time I have carried him down the stairs, kicking my shins and biting my arm, I'm shattered.

I place him down while I get my breath. Chase runs to the front lawn and chucks himself on his side. He does three rolls, then lies on his back, staring at the sky. "Chase, Debbie is in the car. Let's go see Debbie's school."

Debbie starts to bang on the car window, mouthing, "I'm late." After coaxing Chase with toys, I eventually have to lift him again and get him in his car seat. His body goes stiff, and he drops between the car seat and the front seat onto the floor. Four attempts later, he's strapped in and ready to go. I pull off, breathing out a sigh of relief. I get halfway up the street when Debbie shouts, "Mum, stop!"

Looking in my mirror, I see Chase head down in the boot with his legs in the air blocking the back window. I'm on the main road. I look out for somewhere to pull over. A toy car comes flying and smacks me in the nose after bouncing back from the steering wheel. It's so painful, tears roll from my eyes. I find a turn-off to pull into and get Chase out of the boot and into his seat. I eventually get Debbie to school just ten minutes after the bell has gone.

It's been such a struggle, working and managing Chase. I started off doing forty-eight-hour shifts in a residential home that takes on the most challenging young people in the country. I loved that job. I loved the

67

challenge and knowing that I had made a difference. In one weekend, we stopped one girl from jumping off a bridge, one from cutting herself, and had to restrain a sixteen-year-old boy who was smashing up the home. However, when I got back from a tiring forty-eight-hour shift, having had just a few hours of sleep, I was finding that I wasn't the only one worn out.

Mum had been struggling with Chase. She had to stay in the full two days because of Chase not getting in the car and having extreme meltdowns. I eventually had to hand in my notice and get a job in a before and after school club, which became a struggle too. It meant that my mum could have both kids when she finished work, but it also meant we didn't get home until seven, and I didn't see much of Debbie.

I now work in a nursery from nine till four, and Chase attends another nursery full-time, but I worry about him all day. The staff are struggling to manage him and have said that he is a risk to himself, other children, and even his nursery teachers. He jumps on the tables and throws the chairs at children, rolls around throwing any toys within his sight. I don't want him to be punished for something that he can't help. I have spent the last year using time-outs and rewards, but he just gets back up and repeats the behaviour. It's like he just does not learn from the consequences.

I have a full day to go, and I'm already so shattered. I just want to go home and sleep. I try not to think about sleeping and drink my Red Bull quickly before entering the nursery building where I work. Chase is up all night, every night, catching just the odd hour of sleep here and there. A lot of other things have happened in the past two years. Good things, too. After gaining the guardianship order, I met Alan on a night out. Alan is four years older than me and is a chef or was a chef, at least, before he met me. We have just got married in New Zealand, where Alan's cousins live.

We stayed at their house for a month. His cousin and his wife are both counsellors. We pre-warned them about Chase, but I don't think they quite realized just what a challenge they were letting themselves in for. Nobody does until they meet him. You just can't explain it. I laugh, thinking of our wedding photos on the beach, Chase running behind me in the background, trying to pull my veil. I don't know what I would have done without Alan. He's been great. He has taken on so much and has a lot of patience.

He has given up working as a chef and gone to work at a local warehouse so that he can be around to help me out more. I've gained lots more qualifications too over the past year. I have done a diploma in Autism and a diploma in ADHD. Chase has so many autistic traits. He has repetitive behaviour and no sense of danger. He will sit spinning wheels on his bike for hours, yet he can also flit from one activity to another too. He can be very impulsive and takes hyperactivity and inattention to an extreme level.

He's currently under many professionals and is halfway through an Autism assessment at a centre that we attend every week for observations. I've been told that the paediatrician can no longer diagnose ADHD in our area and that a place called CAMHS (Children and young people's mental health services) is the only place that diagnoses ADHD now, but children must be at least six years old, and there is also a two-year waiting list which means Chase would end up being eight by the time he gets a diagnosis.

From my training in ADHD, I can see that Chase meets the full criteria. I also know that it's important to diagnose as early on as possible for a better outcome. So many children just get branded as naughty, loud, and not listening. I don't want that for Chase. He will say sorry right before hitting me. It's like he just can't help himself.

There is no way that Chase will manage school in September. I have his name down for Debbie's school, but I know that I won't even be able to get him through the doors in the mornings. I just can't imagine Chase lining up, sitting at a desk, or even playing with the toys. He throws them at the walls at home and has broken almost every toy we got him for Christmas. Hopefully, we will get him diagnosed at the centre, and they will get him an Education Health Care Plan which is a legal binding document highlighting his needs to help to get him a special needs school in time. I can't see how they could miss his Autism; it's obvious.

I sit with the pre-schoolers now and read a book for group time. It's a break at work, at least. I feel like I'm on edge waiting for another call from his nursery to come and pick him up, but I try to put this worry to the back of my mind and concentrate at work. I can't afford to lose the third job I have had since taking on Chase. It certainly would not look good on my CV when applying for yet another role.

I finish work and notice I have a missed call from Mum. After stepping outside of the nursery building, I ring her back.

"Would you like me to collect Chase from nursery and have him overnight?" It hits me that it is Friday. Gosh, I can't remember the last time I went out on a Friday night or even had a quiet night in with a full night's sleep, for that matter.

"Really? Are you sure? What about the windows? And door locks?" Mum laughs. When I took him to my mum's house last week, he got into her bathroom, locked the door behind him, and turned her taps on full. It took a while to get him out and must have taken her ages to sort out the mess he had made in there. The time before, he swung her cupboard open, taking it off its hinges.

"Your dads took the bathroom door locks off, he's put safety catches on all the windows and gone out to buy a baby listener today, so don't worry. You need a break. I'm having Debbie anyway, aren't I? You and Alan could go out for a meal or something?" I smile. I'm so lucky to have her. I don't know about going out though, a takeaway and a good night's sleep sounds lovely.

I thank her and head home.

When I arrive home, I ring my Auntie Julie. Julie is one of my mum's sisters. Auntie Julie works in a special needs school and is always there to help and advise me when I need to chat about Chase. She answers after the first ring. I tell her all about Chase getting out of his car seat. Auntie Julie tells me that at the special needs school she works at, they have special car seats for the school trips that hold children in and keep them safe. I'm so glad I rang her. I'm going to have to look into these for Chase. I can't keep having him get out of his seat when I'm driving. It's so dangerous.

After hanging up the phone to auntie Julie my mum rings to ask me what the bruises are on Chase's legs. I'm so confused. "What bruises I ask?" Mum explains that there are four round marks each side of Chase's inner thighs that she noticed after picking him up from nursery. I ask her to send me a photograph and gasp as my phone beeps revealing what looks like lots of finger marks from been held down. I have noticed the odd small finger mark on his arm but never anything like this before.

I start to shake. This is why he needs a specialist school that are trained in handling him correctly. I can't wait until Monday, I need to report this now. What if somebody sees them and asks why I haven't reported it?

I can't report it to the nursery though. They are closed now. I ring 101 for some advice. The following day investigating officers are around the house measuring the bruises and taking photographs and notes.

# The centre

We arrive outside of the centre. Today is the day that we have been waiting for. Alan has taken the day off work to be in the meeting, and it's a good job because we would have been late. Chase refused to let me dress him and change his nappy this morning, then did his usual drop to the floor outside the front door and went running for the road. It's been a tough, few weeks. After the police left, they informed social services. We had a full assessment done on us after the report that we made against the nursery. They quizzed my parenting of Chase and looked into both of our backgrounds. It was so degrading. I now have to report this to any jobs I have working with children.

How do I tell a manager that I have been investigated for child abuse? The police did investigate the nursery. Or so they said. The nursery staff told the police that they saw no marks on Chase when they changed his nappy before home time. If only the police had checked the nappy diary and register, they would have seen that the time that the nursery staff gave for nappy changing was incorrect because my mum had picked him up before then. They were clearly covering their tracks.

Maybe they didn't see the marks but they must have been lying about the times to clear themselves. The nursery staff also told them that I was struggling to manage Chase's behaviour. It's so wrong because parents should be able to report their concerns without it backfiring on them. I certainly won't be reporting any marks he comes home with again. How wrong is that? I shouldn't be made to feel this way.

Of course, Chase is a struggle, but I manage him well and certainly don't handle him roughly like that. A shiver runs down my spine as images flash through my mind of Chase's bruising. I breathe in a deep breath. It's time to put that behind us now. We have a new battle to deal with.

"I hope he's got the diagnosis and they agree to a special needs school," I say to Alan. "How will I get him to Debbie's school?" I shudder thinking about carrying Chase up that massive street, kicking and screaming, with all the double-parked cars and hundreds of children around us.

"It won't come to that," Alan says now. "He has developmental delay, and so many Autistic traits, they will pick up on it."

"Hm, I'm not sure," I reply. I don't have much confidence in the professionals here. In the setting where they observe him, it's very much like a special need's nursery.

There are only five children and three child practitioners. He's only there for two hours and plays.

It's not like they have to dress him and get him in and out of the car or go outdoors where it's busy. He's only played up twice. Once, when he refused to come inside from playing and waved a stick at them, which they let him bring into the nursery, and another time when they gave him a bar of chocolate to get him to cooperate.

I know from being a child practitioner myself that chocolate should never be used to get a child to do something. The school wouldn't allow this and certainly wouldn't let him bring sticks into the classroom to swing around. I can't help but feel that by assessing Chase like this, it's not a true picture of him. We walk inside, Alan carrying Chase in his arms. We leave him in the nursery and head to the coffee room where we sit with other parents, waiting for our turn to be shouted in. We all sit nervously waiting. One woman named Sarah, whom I had got to know well since coming here, enters the room red-faced and breaks down in tears. One of the mums puts her arm on Sarah's shoulder.

"I take it it's not gone well," she says.

Sarah tells us how they aren't diagnosing her son. "They have said he's too sociable," she says. "I know there's something wrong. He shows all the other symptoms. I just keep getting put on parenting classes. He can't talk properly and still has speech therapy. They aren't giving him an Education Health Care Plan. I just don't know how he's going to manage without any extra help in school."

I feel for Sarah. She's lovely. We got talking the first time we came here and have become friends. She's been through so much. Sarah is an older parent in her early forties. She has two other grown-up children. You can tell that her son has Autistic symptoms and that it's not her parenting.

"Chase's guardian," they shout now.

I'm filled with dread. We walk into the room to a big table filled with professionals, from paediatricians to educational psychologists. We take a seat at the end. "Has he got a diagnosis?" I blurt out.

"Not exactly," the paediatrician says, "but I've noticed on the records that Chase's birth mum admitted to social drinking during pregnancy. We know that social drinking usually means more than a little. I strongly suspect that Chase has foetal alcohol spectrum disorder known as FASD."

"What? What does that mean? It doesn't make sense. Chase shows clear symptoms of Autism."

"FASD has overlapping symptoms," the paediatrician says now. "It can often look like Autism or ADHD or other disabilities."

"So what happens now?" I say, still not convinced.

She explains that he will be sent to genetics for blood tests that cannot test for FASD but are done to rule out other conditions that can look like FASD.

"Once these are ruled out, FASD will be diagnosed."

I'm so confused. All this time, I have been convinced that he has Autism. The developmental delay, the speech, the behaviours, struggling with parties, and busy places, it all added up. I don't understand how he can have FASD. I have heard of foetal alcohol syndrome but never foetal alcohol spectrum disorder, and I always thought that it was when a baby was born with physical problems and addicted to alcohol.

I can't get my head around it. At least it's simpler, I think to myself. I know kids can have Autism and not get diagnosed until sixteen in some cases. He will simply have a blood test, rule out other conditions, and then she will make the diagnosis.

"So what about school?" I say now. "He's due to start in September, and we need to find him a special needs school."

"Children with FASD manage fine in school," she says now. "It's not until high school that they struggle more, and he won't live an independent adult life."

I burst into tears at hearing this. The thought of Chase not having his own house, a wife, kids, a job.

I stand up and walk out of the room. I head outside for some air, leaving Alan to sit with them. I can't think straight. Alan doesn't follow me out. After ten minutes, I take a deep breath and go back to the building. I see Alan walking out. "They are considering an Education Health Care Plan," he says.

I wipe away a stray tear from my cheek. "How did you manage that?" I laugh.

"I asked them if they are going to take responsibility when Chase or another child gets seriously hurt in school after we have warned them. After a long discussion, the educational psychologist said we could put it all in writing to ask them to reconsider. I don't think the paediatrician was too happy, but the educational psychologist has agreed. Come on," Alan says, "let's go get Chase and get off home."

"You get him," I say, "I will meet you by the car."

I quickly run inside and hand Sarah a piece of paper with my phone number on. She hugs me tightly, and we both promise to stay in touch. I then head towards the car and wait for Alan to bring Chase out. I can't believe what's happening. I think back to my foster care training. I can't remember learning that much about FASD. I have a lot of googling to do when I get home.

# Discovering FASD

"Wow," I say. I've learned so much over the past week. When I got home from the assessment centre, I typed "FASD" into Google, and all these Chase look-alikes popped up. I was stunned into silence. All these children look just like Chase. They have a flat midface, space between the eyes, thin upper lip, smooth philtrum, and upturned nose. How come I haven't thought or heard of this? So many years of training, and I've never come across it. Studies have estimated FASD to be more common than Autism. It often goes undiagnosed or misdiagnosed. I can see why. It looks so much like other conditions. Also, who is going to admit to drinking during pregnancy?

No amount of alcohol is proven safe during pregnancy, yet so many doctors give conflicting information on it. I think back to my pregnancy with Debbie. I can remember one of the midwives telling me a glass of wine is okay. The damage can be done in the early stages of pregnancy. Scary when you think of all the unplanned pregnancies and people that don't find out they are pregnant until six weeks. My heart sinks as I look through a list of nearly four hundred symptoms and conditions caused by drinking.

Not only does alcohol damage the brain, but it can damage other organs too. Bowels are on the list, explaining why Chase has never had a solid poo and suffers from constipation and leaks. Poor balance is also listed. Chase has always had poor balance. It's all finally making sense. It's like all the jigsaw pieces are finally fitting together. Kids with FASD do not understand cause and effect, consequences of their actions. I could cry, when I think of all the times I was telling Chase off and making him sit on time-out. I was punishing him for the damage done to his brain.

I lift Chase now and give him a big cuddle. He has had his blood tests done, and we have sent a lengthy letter off. Hopefully, he will have his diagnosis back soon and get a special needs school in time.

"Are you going to tell Chase's mum and dad?" Alan asks now.

"I think I will leave it for now." I laugh. Over the past two years, Chase's mum and dad have had monthly contact at a local soft play centre. It's been an absolute nightmare. Chase can't handle going out, so it's already a struggle keeping him safe, let alone dealing with his mum and dad swearing at people.

I've had play centre workers coming over to me asking me to calm them down. The other parents have been complaining about them starting fights with people. After his dad asked me to do contact uptown, and I refused due to the number of drug users we get swarming around us whom they know, he called me every name under the sun. Finally, enough was enough, and I sorted out a local contact centre. Ideally, I would have liked it to be just them, which is known as a supervised contact, just like when I was fostering, with a contact supervisor present, but that cost seventy pounds, so I had to make do with a supported contact instead, where they are with other parents and children with contact workers around in the background.

So far, it has not been going very well. The contact supervisors have said Raymond and Rose have been ignoring Chase, sitting on their phones, being loud, swearing, and are struggling to manage him. Last week when my mum and Alan picked him up, his nappy was soaked. They said they couldn't change it. I understand as it's a challenge changing Chase's nappy. Not many people can handle Chase. Then I found out that he had got in the lift and ran around the top floor.

Every time he goes, I'm worried sick about him.

"Is he ready?" Alan says now. I start to put on Chase's shoes when my phone goes. It's Mum.

"Hiya, babe, I'm outside."

"They won't be a sec," I reply. I kiss Alan and Chase goodbye and watch them drive off. I start to get some cleaning done. It's so hard to fit washing, ironing, and cleaning in when Chase is at home. He's always on the go, messing with absolutely everything. I pull him away from one thing, and then he's into something else. I have to supervise him all around the clock. Even running to the loo, I come back to find him up to mischief. Last time he had found one of Debbie's crayons and scribbled all over the living room wall.

Within half an hour, I'm plugging the hoover in when I hear the front door go. I hear Chase come running through the door, and Debbie shout, "Chase, you're back!"

I rush down the stairs. "What's going on?" I say. "Why's Chase back?"

"Debbie, can you take Chase to play in the living room?" Alan asks. I'm filled with dread.

"What on earth have they done now?"

"It's Raymond. He came marching over, screaming in my face," Mum says. Alan and mum tell me about Raymond refusing to pay for the contact, making a scene, and then storming out.

"Where on earth were the staff?" I demand.

"They all stood there stunned," Mum says now.

I'm fuming. Raymond and Rose had been told by the contact centre from the beginning that it's up to the person having contact to pay. "I can't see why I should be the one to pay for their contact. I'm paying to raise their child and struggling as it is," I say.

"Well, Chase was ever so confused," Mum says.

"We had to go in and tell him it was time to leave after Raymond had stormed out. I thought he was going to hit me," Alan says.

I apologize to Mum and Alan. I feel so guilty that they have been put in this situation. I thought they would be safe at the contact centre. "I assume the contact centre has stopped his contact permanently?" I ask.

"I don't know," Mum says. "We just left."

"Well, I won't be putting any of you through that again."

I walk to the kitchen where I left my phone and dial the contact centre number. After four rings, a woman picks up. "Hello," I say. "I'm Chase Groves' guardian." My voice is shaking slightly. "My mum and husband have taken him to contact today, and I hear that there has been an incident."

"Yes, Dad refused to pay us and then went up like a bottle of pop in front of all the children. He was yelling at your husband mainly," she confirms. "Ever so aggressive."

"Well, I won't be sending them and putting them in that situation again," I say. "Can I get it all in writing, please? And will you be the one to inform his dad that the contact has stopped?" I ask.

"Yes," she replies. "I will send you an email and contact Dad to let him know the contact has stopped due to his behaviour."

I thank her and put down the phone. I notice a text.

*If I see you with Chase, I will take him from you—!*

"What's the matter?" Alan says, walking into the kitchen and seeing my face.

"He's threatening to take Chase now."

Mum comes storming into the kitchen. "I'm not having this," she says angrily. "We have done everything for this little boy. You do not deserve this. You have had nothing but grief from social services and now them!"

"You need to contact the police," Alan says, more assertively.

"I will just save the message for now," I reply.

"What a mess." Mum seethes.

My phone rings, violently vibrating on the worktop. I pause, then take a deep breath and answer. It's the contact centre. That was quick. "Hello, is that Lacey?"

"Yes."

"It's Gemma from the contact centre. I'm afraid I have a duty to inform you that a threat has been made towards your husband."

"What," I squeal. "I've had enough of this. You can tell the police. I'm going to report it."

The phone line goes quiet. "Well..." Gemma stutters, pausing again. "It wasn't a direct threat. It was just that if he sees your husband touch Chase again, he will kill him," she says, backtracking.

I put the phone down. I'm so angry I can't speak. "How dare they," I shout. My phone beeps.

*YOU FUCKIN BITCH*

It's written in big block capitals. I type back, my fingers shaking over the keypad.

*I have given up everything for your son. He has brain damage from Rose's drinking in pregnancy. You wouldn't even see him if it wasn't for me, he would have been adopted. I'm sick of the pair of you. Chase deserves better and I'm done with you both.*

I click send. I'm too angry to care. Enough is enough. I ring the non-emergency police number and tell them I want to log a death threat, kidnapping threat, and threatening behaviour. They take some details from me and say they will send someone out later today.

I come off the phone and tell Mum and Alan what's gone on. They are both waiting anxiously for an explanation. "You've done the right thing," Mum says.

"What if I've made it worse? I saw the police records a while back in one of the files I had on Chase. They have no respect for authority, especially the police. They have assaulted police in the past, been done for violence, and carrying weapons. They are dangerous." I turn to Alan. "If they can attack police officers, what can they do to us? They only live five minutes away. What about if I bump into them when I'm out with the kids?"

"Try not to worry for now," Alan soothes. "Let's just wait for the police, see what they can do."

My phone rings again. I quickly answer it without looking at the caller ID.

"Hiya, mate." It's my friend Marie. "Are you okay? Has something happened?"

"Huh?" I pause, confused. "Why? H-how do you know?"

"Do you already know about Facebook?"

"Facebook?" I ask, confused.

"A friend of mine has just rung me. She used to go to school with Raymond's mum and has her on Facebook. She's put a post on saying Chase is getting abused by Alan. I sent you a screenshot."

"Two seconds," I say, looking down at the phone to see a photo showing Chase's mum's name.

*I think the foster carer's husband is beating Chase up, he was covered in bruises...*

That's not all. Below are angry emojis and people commenting. *Ring social services,* one says. *Where does he live?* another one says. I burst into hysterical tears. "Oh my god, I can't do this any more. I've had enough."

Alan snatches the phone. As he reads the snapshot, his face goes red with rage. He lifts the phone to his ear and thanks Marie for letting us know. His voice is still unsteady as he tells her he'll call her later before hanging up.

"I'm so sorry," I say to Alan. "I can't understand why they are taking all this out on you."

"It's certainly not your fault," Alan soothes. It doesn't stop me from feeling guilty, though. So much has happened today. My heart is racing like it's going to jump out of my chest at any minute. We have a long night ahead yet.

# The police

I awake to the sound of the rain patting against the window. It's daylight, and the house is silent. I turn over to see Alan gone. I can hear faint voices coming from downstairs. I reach for my phone under the pillow and tap the keypad. It's ten thirty a.m. How did I manage to sleep in so late? I creep downstairs into the kitchen. Alan is making breakfast. Debbie sits at the kitchen table reading her homework book. Chase crawls across the floor, throwing his teddy at me, and starts to flap his arms.

"Good morning." I smile, stroking his head. "Why did no one wake me?"

"We thought you needed a lie-in." Alan beams. Yesterday's events flicker through my mind when the doorbell rings.

"It might be the police." We waited up until eleven p.m. last night and eventually went to sleep after they didn't show up. I ask Debbie to watch Chase, and we both answer the door, making sure to look through the spyhole first. Two male officers stand fully uniformed. One is in his late fifties, the other looks a bit younger.

"Come through," I say, and we sit down in the living room. "Sit down," I say, pointing to the other sofa.

The older police officer thanks me, taking a seat on the far side of the sofa, and the other says he will stand, staying put in the doorway. I begin to explain yesterday's events, adding the Facebook incident that occurred after I made the police report.

"Can you not get social services to deal with this?" the young policeman says, still in the doorway with his hand on his hip.

I pause, confused. "No," I reply.

I think back to the training I did when the social worker said not to hide our addresses from parents. I can remember wanting to shout out in the group and ask if that applied to the social workers' addresses. I'm sure they wouldn't like to give their addresses out. Thank God I didn't listen and hid my address the best I could.

"Not only are they useless and happy to give out foster carers' addresses, but they are also no longer involved," I explain. "I'm a legal guardian now. Is it not illegal to give death threats, slander someone on Facebook, and threaten to kidnap a child that they have had removed?" I say, trying to hide the frustration that's building up from showing in my voice.

"I understand your concern," the older policeman says sympathetically.

"What am I meant to do then?" I ask. "Simply get a new number and ignore them? What if I see them when I'm out? They will kill me. They are not the type of people to care if they are high on heroin and they have attacked police in the past."

"I wouldn't change your number," the younger one says. "It can frustrate someone more, and it's better that you are aware."

"Yes, I guess," I say thoughtfully.

"As goes for going out. I would just carry on your life as normal. You can't hide away. If you see them, ring us immediately. The thing is, like you say, they have no respect for the law. If we go around to their flat, we can only warn them. Then they will know that you have reported them, and it might put you more at risk."

I feel like my energy is slowly draining. I have no fight left in me. I'm completely deflated. I look at Alan sitting next to me. He hasn't spoken. He looks worn out. I rise from my seat and stand up, indicating that it's time for them to leave. I politely thank the officers, wondering what I am thanking them for, and I see them out.

"What a waste of time!" Alan shouts before the door is even fully closed. We both make our way to the kitchen gasping as we open the door. Most of the contents of the kitchen cupboards are scattered across the floor, the bin on its side. Chase is sat in the middle, surrounded by boxes of cereal, playing with the cornflakes.

"Sorry, Mum. I tried to stop him," Debbie says.

"It's not your fault," I reply as I attempt to clean up, unsure where to begin.

Alan lifts Chase from the floor. "Come on, you little munchkin." He laughs, removing him from the kitchen.

I replay yesterday's and today's events, over in my head. How did it come to this? All that time I spent thinking the battles were over. Little Chase has FASD, and now I've got to be careful wherever we go. There is no way his mum and dad are going to just let it all go. I lean down for the dustpan when my phone rings. It comes up with a private number. "Hello," I mumble suspiciously, hoping it's not Chase's mum and dad with any more threats.

"Good afternoon, my name is Julie. I'm calling from children's services. Is this Lacey?"

"Y-yes," I stutter, confused. "We have had a safeguarding complaint. We have been informed by Chase's dad that your husband—" she pauses and I can hear what sounds like sheets of paper being turned over "—has manhandled Chase. He has an unexplained cut on his head, which Raymond says he asked your mum about, and she and your husband looked at each other like they were covering something up."

"Oh, did he now?" I yell. "Well, I suggest you check with the contact centre. They will tell you, as well as the police, and there may be CCTV footage too. I have had to stop contact and ring the police. They have been threatening us!"

"That is not my concern," she replies sternly. "We will not be speaking with anyone. We will be going in to see Chase at the nursery tomorrow and then coming to see you. We will need to do a child and family assessment, known as Section forty-seven. Do you understand?"

"Of course, I do," I reply. "I'm a child practitioner. I used to foster Chase. I know exactly what Section forty-seven is, but what I don't understand is why you are doing one at the word of an angry parent." I'm so furious, I quickly put down the phone, dropping to the floor in hysterical tears.

I love Chase so much, but I can't live like this. What if this affects Debbie too? I will have this on my record now for life. I'm going to have to explain this in any job interview I have in the future with me working with vulnerable children.

Alan crouches down to me. I didn't even hear him come in.

"What now?" he asks. "Just ignore them."

"It's not just that," I say. "It's social services. Chase's dad has reported us."

"Don't worry." Alan laughs. "It's hardly a surprise. Social services know what they are like, and besides, the contact centre will back us." He smiles confidently.

"Social services don't care about clearing our name," I snap. "They have refused to even speak to the contact centre. They want to assess us. I don't trust them after how they were before. What if they still want to have Chase adopted? They could use this to try again."

"Try not to think about it until they come. We have had such a big weekend. Turn off your phone, and let's go and enjoy the rest of our day with the kids."

"Mum!" Debbie shouts. "Can we go to the park?"

I pause. I just want to sit and mope right now.

"Yes," Alan says. "Come on. Let's go get our coats."

I sigh and force a smile. Alan's right. We need to forget everything. Or at least until the morning, that is.

# Peace at last?

"Good riddance!" I squeal out loud after closing the front door. Today is the last day that we will see the social workers. It's been a tough, few months. We have been quizzed on our ability to take care of Chase and even forced to do parenting classes, threatening that if we don't do them, they won't look into assessing us for the guardianship allowance that we should have been receiving all this time. After joining FASD Facebook pages, I came across special guardianship pages on Facebook too. I couldn't believe it when I saw people complaining that their allowance had been reduced because they are earning more. I wasn't working at all when I took on the guardianship order and was refused, yet people who are working still get it.

I can remember them telling me rudely to go and find a job. After reading up on the guidelines, I was shocked to see that I should be getting it. I started the parenting classes and then found out from a new social worker that it had nothing to do with the guardianship allowance, and I should never have been threatened over it. My application for guardianship allowance was turned down again. The reason was that I get CSA maintenance payments off Debbie's dad for Debbie, and with the tax credits for Debbie too, my income is too high. It still doesn't answer why I didn't get it years ago when I had lost my fostering wage and had to borrow money from my mum and quickly find a job.

Debbie's child maintenance and benefits are for her, not Chase. I can't believe they can include Debbie's money. It doesn't make sense that couples who are both working and earning more money than us get it, yet even when I was single and not working, I couldn't get it. I've complained to my MP and the government ombudsman, but there seems to be nothing they can do as it's guidelines and not a law to pay me. So basically, the local authority can pick and choose whom they pay, and I can't do anything about it.

They don't care that Alan's wage is half of what it should be because he's had to go part time. Last month I cried as I handed in my notice at work. I've been running on empty for so long, and there is no way that Chase is going to get an EHCP anytime soon, so I'm going to end up with him at home because we have no chance of mainstream school coping with Chase. They have been arguing with me that with support Chase will cope in mainstream school. They have no idea, so it looks like it's going to be a case of *I told you so!* It's so cruel that he should be put through that, not to mention the risks to the other children. It's just setting him up to fail.

Chase's mum and dad have stopped with the text messages, although they did report me again. The social worker said that they'd had phone calls off Raymond saying that I had been drinking and taking drugs, throwing wild house parties with Chase. I had to laugh. Rich coming from heroin addicts. I'm too busy looking after their son with foetal alcohol spectrum disorder to have the time for parties. They had been shouting and screaming at the social worker on the phone. She felt very intimidated and had to put the phone down. How the hell does she think I felt then? I've had that face to face for years.

"Anyway," Alan says now, "she's gone, so let's go take the kids out for the day to the beach."

Debbie comes running down the hallway. "Yay, we are going to the beach, Chase."

Chase squeals in excitement and picks up his toy car, throwing it at the windows. It bounces off the window, making a loud bang, causing Debbie to hold her ears.

"You're gonna have to start just leaving teddies out for him and putting the hard toys away, or he will end up putting the windows through," Alan says thoughtfully.

I try to distract Chase with a video on my phone while Alan helps me to change his nappy and get him dressed. Half an hour later, we are all set to go. We arrive at Blackpool beach just after twelve. We are drained from an hour and a half of screaming all the way here. Alan had to sit in the back and try to keep Chase calm. Every time we went past a train, he screamed hysterically, with tears streaming down his cheeks. I don't understand why; Chase loves trains. I think he wants the train and doesn't like it going away. Another trigger for him that I have no power over.

"I hope he's okay, Mum," Debbie says, stroking his face as I lift Chase into his pushchair.

"Don't worry about Chase. He just doesn't like the car, but he will love the beach." Alan reassures her.

As we walk down to the beach, Chase smiles, shouting, "Beach."

"Wow, Mum. Chase said the word beach," Debbie shouts in excitement. I get him out of his pushchair and lay a beach towel out for him. "We have buckets and spades," Debbie shouts, grabbing them from under the pushchair.

Chase snatches the blue bucket and runs down towards the sea, swinging it in the air. "Stop," I shout. The beach is crowded. It's a sunny day, and Chase is weaving in between groups of people, coming in and out of sight. Alan starts to run in Chase's direction. As he passes a line of tents, I lose sight of him too. I feel a rush of panic race through me. My heart rate quickens, and my hands shake.

"He runs fast, Mum," Debbie says. Five minutes pass. I feel like twenty minutes have gone by. I scan around on my tiptoes. Alan comes into sight. He has Chase in his arms, kicking. As he comes closer, I can see he's struggling.

"Chase," I shout. "Thank god you found him."

"He was under a little water bridge with a big sign saying, 'Keep Out'. An elderly couple was asking where his parents were. They said he wasn't responding to them."

"Well, he's safe now," I reply, letting out a deep breath of relief. "He runs so quick, it's impossible to watch him. It's too busy here." We agree to go to a small closed-in park that we passed on the way here. "Reins next time," I shout up to Alan as I trail behind him, carrying Chase.

"Didn't even have time to get them out, let alone put them on." Alan chuckles back as he races up the bank with Debbie on his shoulders, giggling.

When we arrive at the park, it's quiet. It's only small with one swing, one slide, and a roundabout. A man with a small toddler around the same age as Chase walks out the gate as we walk in. Chase and Debbie both run straight for the roundabout, screaming to be pushed. Debbie moves onto the other equipment after ten minutes of being spun. Chase stays, squealing to be pushed some more, for the entire hour we are there. My arms are aching, but he doesn't seem to get bored of going around, nor does he appear to feel the dizziness.

Apart from the usual kick-off when it's time to go, the journey home goes smoothly. Chase sits in his seat engrossed in his toy iPad, pressing the number-five button, flapping both arms out in front of him every time the screen lights up. As I walk through the front door, I stand on something. I look down to see it's a large white envelope. I open it quickly, wondering if it's the diagnosis letter we have been waiting for. I tear it open. I pause, confused. This can't be right. I re-read the sentence.

*We are not diagnosing at this time. I suggest developmental delay is looked into further instead.*

Below it says about Chase's growth not being typical of foetal alcohol syndrome.

"What now?" Alan says, coming in through the door with Chase in his arms and Debbie at his side.

"You're not going to believe this." I squeal. "They aren't diagnosing him because he isn't small."

"A lot of children aren't small, though, are they?" Alan asks, confused.

"No, that's foetal alcohol syndrome that is diagnosed by growth impairment and facial features. If they don't have the growth impairment or specific facial features, it's another term under foetal alcohol spectrum disorder. They are meant to look at the overlapping symptoms, not just growth."

"You did say that not a lot of doctors are fully trained in diagnosing and understanding FASD in England," Alan replies sadly.

"I know I did, but the paediatrician picked up on it, so why is he disagreeing with her? It's a good job I read up on it, or I would have believed this letter, thinking that he can't have it because he's not small."

"What do we do now?" Alan asks.

"Well, these are two different medical opinions we have been given. We will ask for a third."

Later, I go on the FASD support page on Facebook and type out what's gone on, attaching a photo of the letter. People start to comment, putting up angry face emojis at the status.

*You need to request funding for the FASD clinic. Most of the doctors aren't trained. He's going off old guidelines!*

*It took me four years to get a diagnosis, so don't give up!*

This is mad. How can doctors not be trained in a condition caused by drinking in pregnancy? I read a report not long ago on FASD. It was the first FASD study done in this country. It estimated that up to seventeen percent of the population could be affected. Why aren't they doing anything? Training doctors? Displaying posters in doctors' surgeries like they do with smoking?

I go to bed, again feeling completely exhausted. It shouldn't be such a fight to get a diagnosis and support for a child.

# September — school starts

"Get up!" I shout up the stairs to Debbie. "We are going to be late." Today is Debbie's first day back at school and Chase's first day. I'm already worried about how the school will cope with Chase for two hours. That's all that they have offered, so it's lucky I gave up work.

I have to drop Chase off at nine with Debbie and then pick him back up at eleven, then go back to get Debbie at three. It's been a tough, few months with services. We were referred to Children's mental health services (CAMHS) by Chase's nursery. I was sceptical at first, having heard so many things about them putting people in parenting classes, but once I spoke to the disability nurse there and explained the situation, she was lovely. She said we could get MAPA training rather than parenting classes, which would help us with managing Chase's physical outbursts. MAPA is training that a lot of professionals have in safely handling aggressive behaviour so it's a lot more practical than parenting classes.

I have done a lot of more intense training for older children, so it would have been beneficial to do training more suitable for smaller children. She agreed to Chase seeing an occupational therapist for a sensory assessment and also to help us with adapting our home to keep him safe. She agreed that with me being a child practitioner, it would be silly to put me in parenting classes. I was feeling hopeful up until she asked me all the details of services already involved, including the guardianship team from social services, whom I had been referred to after the safeguarding investigation was over.

Weeks later, I am invited to a parenting support group, and MAPA training is refused. An ADHD assessment is refused altogether because I am fighting anyway to get Chase into a special needs school. They asked why I need to label him when I am fighting for a special needs school anyway? I am so angry. He needs a diagnosis for medication. He can barely leave the house without running into the road and throwing himself on the floor, let alone sit still in a chair.

The occupational therapist did visit our home but said that our home was fine as we had already put locks on things ourselves. He wasn't going to do a sensory assessment. He kept asking why we need one. In the end, he reluctantly agreed to do one. The letter arrived this morning. Chase was scored high, showing sensory needs, but then he says in the report that it doesn't take over his life. How dare he? We can't go to the shops. I can barely get him from one place to another. Of course, it takes over his life. He then goes on to recommend a place called Flip Out which is a big indoor trampoline park.

Flip Out is a standard joke in our house as last time we took Chase there, he literally flipped out, hiding under the chairs and screaming hysterically. We had to carry him out, shaking like a leaf. I had explained this to the occupational therapist. He wasn't listening. In fact, he was rude. I can't help but wonder if social services clouded their view of me, giving them a negative attitude towards me. It's funny how CAMHS were nice and offering services, and then all of a sudden, they completely changed after being in touch with social services.

I think we will pay to go private and get our own sensory assessment done for Chase eventually, but for now, we have a private FASD assessment to pay out for, along with a private ADHD assessment. We have been to another clinical genetic team for a third opinion on FASD. The lady we saw said that it sounds like he's got FASD but that she doesn't think we should diagnose it. We then went back to the first clinical genetics team and sent him lots of information on FASD, proving that not all children are small and that Chase does, in fact, meet the criteria for a diagnosis. When we show up, he isn't there.

He has sent a woman who seems higher up to take over. She bluntly asks me what I want before I have even taken a seat. I state that I want a diagnosis for this child because it's brain damage and should not be ignored. She says that diagnosing him would be an injustice and that we should find something else to diagnose him with instead. She is very careful not to answer whether he has it or not. I ask her if she is trained, and she looks offended, stating that all staff are trained, but then when I ask her questions about FASD, she doesn't seem to be able to answer them. I try explaining what I have been learning about the condition, but she doesn't listen. I leave the room, once again feeling deflated. This is the fourth person we have seen.

After giving up and hitting rock bottom, feeling hopeless for a few days, I pull myself together and ask people in the support group if they know anyone who is trained to diagnose FASD. I eventually find a private paediatrician based four hours away. I ring her and book her. We now have two months to get the rest of the eight hundred pounds together for her. We also book an appointment with a private paediatrician just an hour away, whom I find on a Google search. We are hoping she will do an assessment for Chase's ADHD and prescribe medication to help him.

We are going to see her tonight after school. I do not doubt that he will get a diagnosis. I've spent the past few months looking back at my notes from my qualifications in ADHD and Autism. Chase ticks every box and more. Inattention and hyperactivity are at an extreme level. She will probably take one look at Chase and see it straight away when he runs into her room.

But right now, I have school to worry about. Alan was so worried this morning when he left for work that he nearly took the day off. I had reassured him that we would be fine. The last thing we need is for him to be losing a day's pay now that I haven't got a wage coming in.

"Almost ready." Debbie's eyes gleam as she runs down the stairs, grabs her coat from the banister, slips her school shoes on, and bends down to do the buckles.

"Come on, Chase," I say, smiling in an attempt to hide my concerns. "Look, you have a new Teletubbies bag, See."

Chase sits down on the floor and pulls a blanket off the sofa, pulling it over his head, covering his face.

"Are you hiding?" I laugh. I go to pull Chase up. He pulls back, throwing himself onto the rug, hitting his head with a bang.

I slowly go over and stoop down to him. "It's okay," I say. "You are going to play."

Debbie peeks around the door with his toy train. "Look, Chase." Chase jumps up and chases Debbie, running out the front door. Debbie hands the toy over as I scoop Chase quickly into his seat, seeking my opportunity. As we pull out of the drive, Chase unbuckles his seatbelt. I pull over on the fronts and try to buckle him back in, but he throws his body up in the air, making it difficult. On the third attempt, I manage to fasten him in and distract him with a bouncy ball I find on the car floor.

We head to school. Debbie talks to Chase on the way there, trying to keep him distracted from getting out of his seat. We point to cars going past and ask him for the colours of the cars. He replies, "Blue," to one of the cars, and we give him a big clap. When we arrive at school, there is nowhere to park, and I end up a good five minutes' walk away. I unbuckle Chase. As soon as he hears the click, he jumps straight out, barging past me straight into someone's front garden.

"Chase, out." I raise my voice slightly. "Let's have a race," I say, getting into a running position. Chase lies down sprawled on the lawn. I can see a little old lady in her window looking out to see what's going on. I'm filled with dread because I know that if I approach him, he will scream and go stiff, and I will struggle to carry him.

I wish I had brought his pushchair now, but I didn't want school teachers thinking badly of me not being able to manage him. I get enough criticism from social services and the early years professionals from the assessment centre. "Come on, Chase!" I shout again. He doesn't look up at me.

"Mum, everyone has gone in," Debbie says.

"You go on up," I tell her. "Can't have you being late as well."

I watch Debbie walk up the street while pulling a toy from my pocket and flashing it at Chase. He's not looking at me. "Chase, look!" I shout again. "I have a surprise for you."

Chase gets up and walks over to the front window of the house. I quickly race over. I try to pick Chase up, but he flips over on the floor, stretching his body out. I go to lift him, and he scratches my face. The woman bangs on her window. I scoop him up again and run out of the garden, trying to hold the tears back as he pulls hard on a chunk of my hair. I start to walk up the street. I'm out of breath now. He tugs on my coat, pulling it around my neck. My eyes fill with tears that have been building up for so long. I can't do this any more. It's just impossible. I would love to see one of the "professionals" come and do this. They could never deal with this and get him in school, yet they are happy to scrutinize my parenting and give me advice that doesn't work.

In all my years of training in behaviour management, I haven't come across a strategy that works for Chase. Picking him up is getting almost impossible now, and talking doesn't work because he doesn't respond. He doesn't look at me. It's like I'm not here. I stop and place him down while I get my breath back, careful not to take my hands completely off him so that he does not run again. I haven't got the energy to chase him. I lift him again and hobble up the path, him screaming and kicking, slapping me around the head. I just about make it to the school gates where I put him down, breathing a sigh of relief. The gates are locked.

We must be over half an hour late. I ring the buzzer. "Hello, Chase is here," I say, not daring to step away from Chase in case he backtracks down the path.

"OK," the receptionist replies. "Two minutes."

Around five minutes later, I feel like I've been waiting for ages when a teacher and Amanda Burns walk over to us, letting us in. Amanda is from the assessment centre. She's the one with the same qualifications as me who talks down to me and gives me parenting advice. She was one of the staff members who gave Chase chocolate to get him to obey orders rather than sit back and see what he was like in a natural environment like school. "Oh, Chase, you're late," she says, looking accusingly at me.

Memories of that dreadful centre flash to mind, and I can't help but wonder if she will be getting her chocolate out again to coax Chase into school. I wonder how long that strategy will work.

A manager starts to jog over towards the building, turning to Chase. "Come on, Chase. I have toys for you." Chase runs after her. My heart sinks.

*Great! Just typical that he moves for her. Now it's all going to come back to my parenting once again.*

Chase stops suddenly. "Come on," Amanda shouts. He turns his head to the side and spots a slide on the big yard with a little playhouse at the top of it. He runs straight for it, climbing up to the house, and sits in it, looking down at us all.

I can't help but feel smug. *Come on then, Amanda,* I think. *Let's see you coax him out now.* I try not to laugh as Amanda starts talking up to Chase. The class teacher offers to get some toys from the classroom. I thank her as she walks around the back of the school building where the nursery room is. I feel like going up there and trying to get Chase. I'm struggling to stand back, but I'm adamant about letting her see how hard it is to deal with Chase and watch her strategies fail.

The class teacher comes out with a selection of toys, one of them a little blue train. "Chase, come on, now," Amanda shouts up. "I have a toy train look." Chase looks down blankly at her, not budging. "Well," Amanda says, "we will sit here and not acknowledge him until he gives up and comes down."

"Okay," I say, taking a seat and hiding my grin. This is going to be a long wait. He's only meant to be doing from nine until eleven, and it's twenty to ten already.

I sneak a look up at the playhouse. Chase has gone inside it, now out of sight. "You see, Lacey," Steph says. "We just need to show him some authority and not give in to his demands. He will soon come down."

I sit back and relax in silence. I can see Amanda getting agitated, ready to get up. We sit for several minutes. "Right, it's nearly ten o' clock," she says eventually after a long wait.

She goes over to Chase and sternly asks him to come down. Chase comes down the slide. "Well done," Amanda says, pleased as Chase walks towards her. He dodges around her and runs for the climbing frame. Amanda's face turns red. "No, Chase," she says sternly, walking over to him. Chase climbs up the frame, then crawls through the gap and jumps down. He's on the inside of it now. There's no way she can fit through there to get him out. A laugh slips out, and I quickly raise my hand to my mouth, pretending to cough.

Amanda tuts at me, shaking her head. "Right," she says, "I've gotta leave soon. I've got an appointment, and I'm going to be late. I was only meant to be coming in for the first hour."

I can't help but feel angry. How the hell does she think I manage when I have an appointment and Debbie too? This is my daily life, and she can't even do it for one morning but wants to give *me* tips. How dare she!

"Right." She sighs again. "You're gonna have to pick him up."

"Go on then," I challenge, staying put. My face is red with anger. I'm not having this. I look up at the school towards the headteacher's office and see the principal, Mrs Ferns, standing staring out of the window. I wave up at her and shrug my arms at her in a gesture to say, *Look at this. I told you so.*

Amanda tries to put her hand through the climbing frame. Chase crawls out. Amanda stoops down to lift him. As she goes to grasp him, he slips straight through her arms, dropping to the floor. She attempts a second time, and he kicks her in the knee, dropping back to the floor, rolling on his side. "You're going to have to get him, Lacey," she says now.

"I hope you are going to be putting all this in your reports," I say. "This is exactly why he needs a special needs school. He hasn't even made it through the doors."

111

"I don't have to put everything in my report," she replies.

I can't believe what I am hearing. "You do know that you have just physically intervened with Chase. That warrants an incident form," I correct, thinking back to my work in the children's homes.

"I have got to go," Amanda says, now walking off the premises. I turn around to see the teacher has gone back to class.

"Come on, Chase." I laugh. I can't believe what has just happened. I take a deep breath and lift Chase. I carry him back to the car. He doesn't make as much of a fuss as he had on the way up.

I put him in his seat and head for home. "Home." Chase smiles. When we arrive back at the house, Chase tips over the toybox and sits on the floor, spinning the wheels on his toy car. I take a rare opportunity to quickly get some cleaning done. My mum picks Debbie up from school for me and brings her home. It's a good job that she works in a school kitchen and finishes work at two thirty, or I would be stranded at school unable to collect Debbie.

Alan arrives home from work shortly after. We quickly pick up all the paperwork that we have spent all weekend photocopying and head off to the private hospital for Chase's appointment. "I hope she diagnoses him," I say to Alan.

Alan laughs. "Come on, she's not going to miss his ADHD. I told you before."

When we arrive at the clinic and get Chase out of his car seat, he stands by the side of the car, waiting. I hold his hand, and he lets me, strolling nicely across the car park. Alan chuckles.

"It's not funny," I snap, unimpressed. "I can't remember the last time he walked nicely without being carried. I can't think of even a single occasion."

"Don't worry," Alan says, seeing my frustration. "Typically, kids behave on the one occasion you want them to show it."

"Hm," I reply. As we walk through the doors, I see a little reception desk. It's so quiet. There are only a few men in their late fifties waiting on the sofas quietly. It's so posh. "I feel a bit out of place," I whisper.

Chase shouts, "Hiya! Hiya!" He comes to life as he runs to the desk, grabbing a pile of leaflets and throwing them one by one across the floor.

Alan quickly holds his hands, removing the remaining leaflets from his grasp. I quickly pick up the leaflets and place them back, apologizing to the lady on the reception desk. She doesn't look impressed. I drop my head in embarrassment. "We have an appointment with Dr Garna, a children's paediatrician," I say, handing her the appointment letter.

"Take a seat," she replies, looking over her glasses, flicking her long light-brown hair back as she spins back around in her chair to face the computer.

Chase runs in circles around the sofa, squealing playfully until we are eventually called through. Dr

Garna is a slim Asian lady in her late fifties with long black hair scraped back into a ponytail. She offers us a seat. We look hesitantly at Chase. "Don't worry, he's fine," she says.

"Chase, do you want to colour at the table?" She puts a colouring book down on a little red plastic table with a selection of crayons and pulls out a seat.

"Chase, come and sit down." Chase doesn't respond. He runs over to the patient's bed, looks underneath, and starts messing with the screws. He notices the wheels and starts to spin them.

"Leave him," she says as she takes a seat. We hand her a thick folder of paperwork, and it hits her desk with a bang. She starts to look through with a highlighter. There's a silence between us for the next ten minutes while she concentrates. "Wow," she says, eventually looking up. "I don't think anyone has brought me so much paperwork before." She smiles. "Why on earth hasn't this boy got a diagnosis?"

I begin to explain that CAMHS refused to look at ADHD, not just because he's too young but even in the future because he will hopefully be in a SEN school anyway.

"That's ridiculous," she says. "Look." She points out what she has highlighted in the report from the assessment centre. "'Chase does not respond; his attention is flitting'." She points to the second page. "'He won't sit at the desk and is full of energy, unable to concentrate.' Throughout this report, they are saying he has ADHD without putting the diagnosis on it." She tuts, confused.

I feel so relieved for the very first time. A professional can finally see what I can. "What happens next?" I ask.

"Well, I don't think he will even sit for my inattention tests." She laughs. "Judging by this report, I will send out questionnaires for home and school and look at the scores from them first." She pauses, looking over at Chase, who is clicking the plug socket switches on and off. Luckily, they are covered.

"My impression is Autism." She looks up at us.

I could cry with relief. "I've said that from the very beginning. He has developmental delay, communication issues, repetitive behaviours, he's scared of parties and flaps his arms in excitement when he sees the doors open and close."

"Not to mention the escalators," Alan adds.

"He's already had the Autism assessment, though," I explain. "The outcome was that he may have FASD. We are taking him for an assessment soon because different doctors gave different opinions. They haven't got a clue."

"There's not enough training on FASD," Dr Garna replies. "A lot of children with FASD have many other diagnoses under it, ADHD and sometimes even Autism. You may end up getting many different diagnoses over the years," she says. "We need to look at the ADHD first and treat it with medication, then look into the other diagnoses after. Without treating the ADHD, he won't be able to take the assessments. The hyperactivity is extreme, isn't it?" She smiles.

I look over at Chase. He's rolling back and forth across the floor, kicking his legs in the air.

When we come out, we book another appointment for in a month's time and make our way to the car. Alan is carrying Chase, chucking him up in the air to distract him. "Can you believe that?" I ask.

"I told you they were all a waste of time," Alan replies. "It's wrong that we should have to pay to go private, but it's the only way, and he deserves answers and understanding. I'm going to ask work if I can swap shifts again and do the school shift," Alan says.

"Erm, I don't think so," I state stubbornly. "I can cope fine, and besides, we need the money."

"I don't think we have much choice. It's only a matter of time before he's kicked out of that school! You can't carry him in as it is. He needs two of us, and Debbie needs one of us too. You can't take Debbie to school when you're dealing with Chase."

"I've already lost my job," I say sadly. "My career is gone. Years of training wasted, and now you're dropping even more hours again?"

"We will be okay," Alan reassures. "Hopefully, we will get tax credits. I know it's not as much, but we will get by."

We pull off and head for home. I feel so relieved. Chase will finally have a diagnosis. I can stick up for him.

He's not naughty, and I'm not a bad parent, and Amanda Burns and her strategies are not going to cure him. It's about time everybody accepted his disabilities and met his needs. He's going to need a special needs school and a lot of support. I also can't help but worry how on earth we are going to afford all these private assessments and medication, especially now only one of us is going to be working part time.

# The meeting

I sit still, feeling anxious. Nine others sit around the table, chatting away. I have been dreading this meeting, but the school staff thought an Early Help meeting would help. The school has been supportive. Most mornings after dropping Chase off in the nursery room kicking and screaming, the school special educational needs coordinator has invited me into the office for a cup of tea and a chat. It's been great to offload. She has said that Chase needs a special needs school and that it's wrong how the local authority has put him through this, knowing he's a risk to himself and others.

Last week, Mrs White told me that they had to evacuate the entire class when Chase became hysterical, hurling toys across the room. She said that never in her twelve years of working at the school did she see such an outburst. I felt awful, but she assured me that it was not my fault. It was never my intention to put people at risk, and I am still fighting so hard to get him moved to a school with fewer children and more staff who are equipped to deal with him. Hopefully today, with two social workers from the guardianship team, Amanda Burns, a manager from the Early Help team, and the health visitor, we can work together to get Chase moved.

Mrs White starts off reading out the reason why we have been referred for Early Help. She explains Chase's severe outbursts and the struggle I am having getting him in in the morning. She then goes on to explain the incidents when Chase has been in people's gardens before school and when I have had to restrain him from running into the road on several occasions to protect him from oncoming traffic. She mentions an occasion when Chase threw a hard toy that hit Debbie, leaving her eye marked. She then goes on to explain how we struggle to push Chase down into his car seat to get his straps around him and that he keeps getting out.

When she's finished reading, the room falls silent. They all turn in my direction, looking at me sympathetically. The health visitor is the first to break the silence. "Well," she says, "that's just awful! I think we are all hearing this and wondering what we can do for you."

"I'm fine." I smile. "We love Chase, and he's worth every second. Alan has gone part-time at work now, and we are doing the school runs together. We just need Chase to go to a special needs school, where he will be less anxious and have all the support he needs and hopefully transport too. I know children who attend a special needs school have a bus to pick them up. That way, we can just worry about getting Debbie to school and have a break in the day, knowing that Chase is safe and looked after. He's only able to do two hours at the minute, and one day, we will need to return to work."

"Why do you think a special needs school is any different?" the manager from Early Help snaps across the table.

I'm taken aback, and for a minute, my mind goes blank before I reply. "Well, transport for one, as they have trained staff on the bus, so hopefully, he will go in easier. They are trained in physically handling children, and Chase has serious outbursts needing someone to hold him to keep him safe. But hopefully, he will be calmer in a quiet room with fewer children. He's struggling with so much going on. We don't have lots of toys out at home. We keep our house to a minimum. He still has outbursts but not quite as many as at school. He's only able to come for two hours a day."

"We can only have him for two hours," Mrs White states, "as our school's one-to-one support can only sit in with him for two hours."

"You won't get transport anyway." The Early Help manager butts in again. "A special needs school will not do anything different. I used to work in one, so I know what I am talking about. He will be fine in the mainstream."

I want to shout and scream at her across the table. *He's in for two hours because they can't manage.*

"Why does he not have loads of toys at home?" she questions me now.

"Excuse me?" I say, looking at her, wondering if I am hearing right.

"Well, all children need choices," she retorts.

"Well, actually," I explain, "children with FASD need to be parented differently due to the brain damage. He can't cope with too many toys and choices. It overloads him."

"Well, he copes fine at school," she responds sternly.

I look towards Mrs White and the principal, Mrs Ferns, waiting for them to step in and tell her how much he's struggling. They both catch my eye and look away. Mrs White puts her head down.

My heart sinks. I feel so betrayed. Mrs White understands and knows that the school can't cope for two hours with him. Why is she not stepping in?

"What's happening with parents' contact?" one of the social workers shouts out. All eyes turn to me. I try to steady my shaking hand. My mind has gone blank again. I thought that they were going to help.

"Chase's dad threatened us," I say. "He's so aggressive. We can't even go out in case we bump into him."

"You need to think about Chase rather than yourself," the Early Help manager shouts out again. She's a rather large lady with short hair in her late fifties. I'm not sure if I have ever actually met her before or if she's met Chase, for that matter. I know he's under the early years and gets discussed at meetings.

"I am thinking about Chase," I respond. "How dare you!" I can feel my anger building up, and I'm struggling now to keep it out of my voice. I just want to cry. I came here for help, and I feel like it's become a witch hunt. A chance for them to all bully me around a table.

"We will set up mediation for you," the social worker says smugly from across the table.

"Have you forgotten that your social workers wouldn't even be near them because they were all too scared, running from court?" I snap. "Yet you want me to put my life at risk with a heroin addict who, according to his record, carries knives and assaults police! If you want contact, then you can do it!"

I'm shaking now. I can no longer hold back, and I can feel everyone staring smugly at me. I need to get out. I need to leave. I can't do this. I'm going to break down in tears, and then they will be accusing me of not coping. I pray the meeting hurries up and comes to an end.

"You have the SGO, so we can't do contact," the social worker states now.

"Well, he should have been adopted, and then he wouldn't need contact in the first place," I reply.

The early year's manager speaks out again. "I'm rather concerned about you restraining Chase."

"Would you like me to let him run on the road?" I ask, my agitation showing in my voice.

"No, you should be talking to him and using strategies." I look across at Amanda Burns. She knows she couldn't talk him into moving herself. The school and Amanda know what he's like. Why is no one speaking up? I look around the table. Amanda and the school staff are looking away, as is the health visitor.

I look the social workers in the eye. "There is something that you can do. Chase needs a special needs car seat in the car that he can't get out of as he keeps jumping out whilst I'm driving. Now that is a serious concern." I raise my arms and draw sarcastic quotation marks in the air with my fingers. "They cost seven hundred pounds that we don't have with both of us quitting work and social services not paying any SGO allowance, so maybe you could help with that. I have found a charity myself; I just need you as a social worker to sign the application form and vouch for his needs."

"I can't do that. It's not my job," the social worker replies.

"So, you are a social worker and talk about keeping children safe, yet you won't sign a form so that I can get him a safety car seat? Are you for real?"

"Maybe your doctor can help?"

The social workers and Early Help manager question his FASD. "He hasn't been diagnosed." The Early Help manager sniggers. The room eventually goes silent.

Mrs White finally starts to speak. I wait in anticipation for her to explain Chase's unmanageable behaviour. Instead, she thanks everybody for coming, looks at her watch, and tells me it's time to collect Chase. She opens the door for me, and everyone else stays seated. I don't argue. I step out of the room and storm down the corridor breaking into hysterical tears that have been building up for the past hour.

The class teacher comes out to me and rubs my back. She shouts out to the other teacher to give me a minute. "I'm a child practitioner myself," I say through tears. "I could have worked in schools or done their jobs lecturing parents, but instead, I went into fostering to help. I don't deserve this, I'm just trying to help him. Why is nobody listening?"

She remains silent and starts to gather Chase's school bag and other belongings. I walk over to Chase, putting on a brave smile. "Come on, Chase, I have a treat in the car," I say, silently praying he comes out with me. I don't want a fight today. I need him to leave. Thankfully, he walks out of the building with me. The school teachers remain quiet. I ring my mum. As she answers, I struggle to get my words out.

"What on earth has happened now?" she shouts. "I'm outside school waiting for you."

"I'm coming," I say, putting down the phone. As I walk out onto the street, I see my mum is standing outside her car on the corner across from the lollipop lady. Her face is filled with rage.

"What on earth has happened?"

I let it all out as she belts Chase into my car that is parked next to hers.

"Get him home," she says.

"But what about Debbie?" I ask.

"I'm getting Debbie, and then I will meet you at home!" She storms across the street.

I hope she's not going to go in and make a scene, but I haven't got the energy to protest. I make my way home. Alan comes out to help me in with Chase. "What's happened?" he asks. "Did your meeting go okay?"

I repeat today's events. Alan is furious. I'm just numb. I don't think I have any fight left in me any more. I lie on the sofa and sob silently. In the kitchen, I can hear Chase screaming and banging the freezer. Alan explains to Chase that the food in the freezer isn't cooked, and it will make him poorly. Chase continues to bang the door as Alan tries to distract him by offering him crisps and things in the fridge. He's set on the freezer food and continues to scream. Several minutes later, everything goes quiet. I pull myself off the sofa and reluctantly go into the kitchen. Chase is sitting at the table, shovelling cake into his mouth, bits falling all over the floor.

"I have put the kids' tea in," Alan explains, but I've let him have a little piece of cake before tea; otherwise, he was going to eat frozen peas." Alan laughs.

"That's fine." I laugh back numbly. "My mum should be home by now. I just hope she's not kicking off. You know what social services are like. They will be accusing her of being aggressive and all sorts if she has gone in there angry.

"Your mum's hardly aggressive!" Alan laughs.

"Well, that sure doesn't stop them from writing it in their reports," I reply.

Twenty minutes later, there's still no sign of my mum. Debbie finished school a while ago. She should be back by now. My phone rings from the hallway. I rummage in my coat pocket for it and quickly answer without looking at the caller ID. "Hello, Lacey," a voice says. The phone goes silent. I recognize the voice immediately. It's the Early Help manager who has been shouting at me all afternoon.

"What?" I reply, shaking.

"Well, you know yourself as a child practitioner–" she pauses "–that I have a duty to report safeguarding issues."

I freeze. "What safeguarding issues?"

"I have reported you for restraints!"

I'm sure I can hear the sniggers in her voice. "Okay," I reply. "Well, good luck with that one. I'm trained in them and am entitled to use them if Chase's life is in danger. Besides, social services have known for months that I have had to physically stop him from hurting himself." I put the phone down and burst into tears again.

Alan comes running in to hear the conversation. The doorbell rings. Alan goes back out of the living room to the door. "It's your mum and Debbie," he shouts, letting them in.

Debbie comes running over to me. I cuddle her, and she makes her way into the kitchen to sit with Chase.

"What have you done?" I ask Mum accusingly, dreading what I'm about to hear.

"I turned up, and social services were still there talking to the school staff," she replies angrily. "I walked in and asked them what the hell they were playing at. I told them that this boy has FASD, and my daughter has done nothing but help him."

"Oh no," I tut.

"I hope you haven't made it worse." Alan laughs, looking at my mum, waiting for her to finish.

"Well, they asked me why Chase needs a diagnosis, and then they said that they were referring him to see if he has attachment issues. So I asked them, 'Why are you referring to him for that?' They said to find out if he has it, so I said, 'Well, that's why Lacey is looking into FASD, to see if he has that, as that is brain damage and cannot be cured.' I told them that my daughter has done nothing but try to get Chase some support. She puts the support in at home and just wants a school that can do the same there."

"I can't believe social services were still there so long after I left," I say, worried. "School has been so good, and now social services have turned them against me just like they probably did with CAMHS. What the hell am I going to do? I have another safeguard now..."

"What?" Mum shouts, going red with rage.

"Just leave it, please."

"But it's disgusting, why have they got it in for you so much? Is this because you took them on in court?" Mum asks.

"Wouldn't surprise me," I agree.

My phone rings again, flashing up the dreaded private number. "Here we go again." I tut, picking it up.

"Hello, is that Lacey?"

"Yes," I reply, feeling that familiarity once again.

"We have had a safeguarding complaint made against you."

"I know," I reply. "This is all because I agreed to a so-called Early Help meeting that turned into a witch hunt. Well, don't worry. I won't be doing that again."

"Are you stopping the Early Help?" she asks.

"Well, I've just been bullied across a table, so what do you think?"

"If you are stopping the help that's been put in place, then we have serious concerns. You either keep working with the guardianship team, or it's a child and family assessment," she replies.

I put the phone down and ring the social worker who attended the meeting with her manager for the Early help. "What's this about safeguarding concerns?" I ask as she picks up. "You do realize that Chase is disabled, and I'm not the only one needing to physically hold him? Amanda Burns did the other day, and now she has left it out of her report. I questioned her about it, and now conveniently, that early years' manager, whom I believe to be her manager, has reported me. What a coincidence."

"The safeguarding team will be able to help you more than we can," she replies. "It's not a bad thing that you're under safeguarding."

"I shouldn't be under safeguarding," I reply. "I have done nothing but protect this child. It's a clear vendetta. If there were concerns around these restraints, then why haven't you done safeguarding assessments yourself? You know we have to hold him. You have known for ages,"

"Well, like I said," she replies, "We have had a complaint, so we have to follow it up." The safeguarding team will be out after school on Monday, okay?"

"They said it wasn't a safeguarding concern unless I refuse to let you work with us?"

"You're under safeguarding, I've been told."

"Fine," I say, putting the phone down. I turn to Alan. "What the hell are we going to do?" I ask.

"Don't worry, we will sort this," Alan soothes.

"Debbie is at risk too because of all this." I cry.

Mum tuts, walking into the kitchen.

I wonder yet again what I have done to deserve this? This is going to be another safeguarding investigation on my record now. This could destroy my career. If I ever try to work again, I'm going to have to declare all this. A scarier thought now comes to mind. What if I ever have another baby? It will be picked up on the midwife's system, and they could automatically become involved.

It suddenly occurs to me that the day I took social services to court, I put my career, my children, my everything on the line. How far will they take this safeguarding investigation? Will they use them all to make a case against me? Oh god! What have I done? But what option do I have? I cannot let my little boy go.

# The undercover safeguarding visit

We sit waiting. Alan looks at his watch. It's five o'clock, and there's still no sign of the safeguarding team. They emailed over the weekend, ordering us to be in for four. Alan took another day off work to prepare for the visit. In the middle of the table sits a Dictaphone and a disclosure form for social services to sign to agree to the meeting being recorded.

I did not sleep a wink Friday night due to worrying. All I could picture was social services lying to take Chase away from us. Saturday morning, we agreed to buying a Dictaphone and only allowing social services to discuss the latest safeguarding if they agree that the discussion can be recorded. I feel reassured that they won't be able to say things that have not been said, but I'm still worried in case they refuse to be recorded. If I refuse to let them in, then what will happen? What if they accuse me of being obstructive? Can they get a court order to come in?

You would think families would be entitled to protect themselves from information being fabricated against them. The police come to mind again, and I ask myself the same question I've asked before. If police interviews are recorded, then why aren't safeguarding meetings? If people are entitled to solicitors in an interview, then why not a safeguarding meeting? These are children who need protection.

The doorbell rings. I look at Alan. "You go," I say. Alan gets up and makes his way to the front door.

"Oh, hiya," I hear him say. The lady from the guardianship team and her manager come strolling in. Her eyes scan around the kitchen, stopping on the Dictaphone. She glances at the pile of papers and folders set out.

"I thought the safeguarding team was coming?" I say, confused.

"Safeguarding? What safeguarding?"

"You…" I pause, even more confused.

"I have no idea what you are talking about, Lacey. We are here to assess Chase for some services from the adoption fund that he may be entitled to."

She glances back over at the Dictaphone and takes a seat. Then it hits me. She's suddenly being nice and changing her tactic because she thinks the Dictaphone is already recording her. It looks like our safeguarding has gone, and they are going to help. How cunning though, denying any knowledge of safeguarding. She knows exactly what she said on that phone call. I wonder how spiteful they would have been if that Dictaphone wasn't there to scare them into doing their jobs at last?

I can hear Mum in the living room playing with the kids. There's a moment of silence.

"Well," she says, "how are you all?"

"F-fine," I reply in amazement. We start to talk about Chase and his difficulties.

The manager then asks, "So what's happening with restraints?"

I laugh. I can't help it. "I thought this wasn't a safeguarding visit. But as you ask..." I hand over two sheets of paper to her. One is a photocopy of my certificate in restraining techniques, and another is my written work from my therapeutic residential support training. It explains the definition of restraint and how and when it should be used. It also explains the laws around using restraints. "As you can see," I say, "I am perfectly within my rights to keep Chase safe. Restraint can be used when someone is putting themselves or others in danger. I think Chase qualifies, don't you?"

They both look at each other. "Do you mind if we look upstairs?" one of them asks. When she sees my facial expression, she quickly adds, "For our disability assessment. We are looking at the adaptations you have made."

I wonder if they are looking to see if we have locks on the bedroom door. I remember from working in the homes that the children are to be locked out, not in. You can have locks on cupboards and rooms with dangers in but not on children's doors.

"Come up," I say, leading the way. I show her the locks on my door. I see the curiosity on her face as she turns towards Chase's room. "No lock on children's doors," I say, showing both sides. Her face drops. It's like she's disappointed. It hits me that they are generally in search of anything they can use against me.

I lead her back downstairs, watching the look between both social workers as she discreetly shakes her head. The other social worker starts to gather her belongings. I've never known a visit so short.

"Thank you for seeing us." She smiles, glancing again at the Dictaphone.

Alan leads the two of them out. I stay seated, a sense of relief washing over me. I hear them saying bye to Chase and then hear Chase running after them, shouting at them to stay, trying to tell them all about his Teletubbies.

I hear my mum trying to distract him now. The front door eventually closes. "The sneaky buggers." Mum seethes, coming into the kitchen.

"You heard then?" I laugh.

"Let's hope we have seen the back of them," Mum says. The reality is that with Chase's disabilities and us now being under these silly Early Help meetings that we can't stop this. We are always going to be under their radar. One wrong word and they will be back. I'm always going to be living in fear of another safeguarding visit. I'm always going to be watching over my shoulder. For now, though, we can relax. It's time to enjoy time with the kids. Tomorrow we have another big day ahead.

# A diagnosis at last

We arrive outside the school gates. Debbie runs straight up to the top yard to join her class, who is starting to line up. Chase is carried once again in Alan's arms. "He's getting heavy," Alan laughs.

"Must be all that milk he has in the morning and before bed." I laugh back. The headteacher, Mrs Ferns, comes out to meet us with Mrs White by her side.

"Hello, Chase," Mrs White says, looking straight at him and avoiding my eye contact. Mrs White pulls out a finger puppet from her jacket pocket and starts making funny voices at Chase. He looks straight past the teachers, and spotting the chickens, he runs straight towards them.

"See you soon," I say, turning to leave. Mrs Ferns nods her head and turns away towards Mrs White, who is already chasing Chase up the path.

It's like they just can't look at me since the meeting and whatever social services said about me. They have completely turned against me like all of our conversations never happened. Alan and I walk back down to the car and head off to the pub for breakfast. When we arrive, we take a seat and order two Cokes and two full English breakfasts. I check my phone, mindful of the time. We only have just under an hour until we need to pick Chase back up from school and head down to Manchester to see his private paediatrician. I flick the side button to check it's on loud.

"Relax," Alan says. "Chase is fine. School can manage him."

"Hardly," I reply.

"Hm, maybe not," Alan agrees, "but that's their problem. They should have spoken out and got him moved. Leave them to it!"

"I'm nervous about today too," I admit. "What if she hasn't got enough evidence to diagnose him? If the private paediatrician can't make a diagnosis, then no one ever will."

"There is no way he won't get an ADHD diagnosis today," Alan soothes. "Even if the school has made out he's not hyperactive there, she's seen it for herself. Things are finally going to start going right for us."

The waitress leans in. "Two full English breakfasts?" She places them down on the table. "If you need anything else, just let me know."

"Thank you." I smile. We start to eat our breakfasts when my phone rings.

"Leave it," Alan tuts.

"It could be school," I say, picking it up.

"Can you pick Chase up, please?" It's Mrs Ferns.

"Why?" I ask.

"He's having a massive tantrum, throwing everything at the children."

"Oh dear," I reply, "won't be long."

Alan's looking over, waiting for an explanation. "Not school?"

"Yep." I laugh. "Surprise, surprise, they can't manage."

"I have no sympathy," Alan retorts, and we carry on eating.

When we have finished, we pay the bill and head off. Pulling up outside school, we reluctantly ring the buzzer on the front gates. They must be waiting because they pick up straight away and buzz us in. Mrs Ferns is waiting in reception.

"I am going on holiday next week, and I have to say I am worried about what will happen while I'm away."

Finally, I have waited so long for this moment. I can't believe what I'm hearing. After everything, they are finally admitting it. I want to shout. I want to ask her why on earth she couldn't simply have been honest from the start. Why she couldn't have saved me from all the stress, all the safeguarding visits, and all the fights?

Instead, I hold back and wait for her to continue, enjoying the moment that I've been longing for. "I have rung the special needs school, and Chase will be starting on Monday. I know the head teacher there."

"But what about the local authority?" I ask.

"He can't stay here. I will sort it," she confirms.

I thank her. Despite everything, I'm grateful she's finally moving Chase, even if it is for her own sanity rather than listening to us in the first place.

We skip out of the building, smiling. No more carrying Chase up this street kicking and screaming. "I told you today would be a good day." Alan beams. Chase runs, giggling, to the car. It's as if he knows this torment is finally over. "Look what I have," Alan says, handing Chase his iPad while strapping him in his seat.

We head off on our hour-long journey feeling positive at last. By the time we pull into the car park, Chase is screaming and crying. He's had enough and has hurled his iPad backwards into the boot.

"It's okay, It's okay. We are here now. Let's go find the toys," I say, lifting Chase out. He drops to the ground and starts to bang his head on the concrete floor. I quickly sit behind him, lifting his head onto my belly, pulling him up until Alan comes and lifts him sideways across his chest in a baby position.

I gather his changing bag and the folder with paperwork in and lock the car. As we carry him through reception, all eyes turn to us. Chase is screaming now to be put down. I can just read their thoughts. *Why are they carrying him at his age? Put that child down!* I know that the minute Alan puts Chase down, he will either run back out of the door or just roll across the floor, and we won't get anywhere. We race to the lift. Chase screams to press the button. Alan lets him go down and press it.

When the lift opens, Chase runs inside and presses all the numbers. The lift stops on the first floor, and we get out, lifting Chase and placing him back down. Chase sees Dr Garna and immediately recognizes her. He runs straight at her.

"Hello, Chase. He remembers me," Dr Garna says, guiding us into her room. She sits at her desk, offering us seats across from her, and starts to flick through a heap of paperwork on her desk, a look of seriousness on her face. She begins to mark the paper.

It looks like the questionnaires she sent to school. I try to sneak a glance at the answers, but she turns the pages. "Well, it's quite clear Chase has ADHD," she says, "and foetal alcohol spectrum disorder too."

"Has he got an ADHD diagnosis?" I ask.

"Yes, these scores show ADHD. The school has scored him high in all three areas."

"Really?" I am surprised. "Is it an actual diagnosis though," I ask now.

"Well, yes, of course," she reassures. "I'm diagnosing FASD too."

I could cry with relief. Not only is she diagnosing ADHD, which is what we have come here for, but she has also picked up on his FASD. I will need to cancel his FASD appointment when I get home which will save us eight hundred pounds that we can't really afford in the first place.

"Thank you so much," I say now.

"I'm just shocked no one diagnosed him sooner," she replies. "All the evidence is in the paperwork you gave me. Now, have you thought about medication?"

"I tried before and got accused of sedating him." I laugh, thinking back.

"They usually have to be a bit older," Dr Garner explains, "but I have a special licence. Chase is a severe case. He needs medication to calm down the hyperactivity."

We agree to start him off on the minimum amount and see how he gets on. We come out relieved. "I can't believe it, Alan," I say. "He's got an ADHD and FASD diagnosis. At last, its acknowledged after all that."

"Finally," Alan agrees. "He has a new school to go to and two diagnoses now.

"He's no longer adoptable to social services now," I state. "Maybe they will leave him alone."

"Maybe," Alan says, not too convinced, "but I think it's more than wanting him for adoption now. It's become a vendetta that's got out of hand."

"Well, now we have the diagnoses for them to argue with. They can't try to blame my parenting any more, so let them find something else to try to fight me with."

"Let's just get home and celebrate for now," Alan says.

"I agree," I reply, feeling relieved and hopeful at last. I contact my friend Amy whom I met on an online support group for FASD. Amy has been amazing. She saw my posts about safeguarding investigations and struggles to get a diagnosis and privately messaged me. We have become friends. Amy is a retired social worker. After adopting several children and fostering, she decided to train as a social worker to make a difference in the system. Social services placed a child who had raped another child in his previous foster home with her and her children and didn't tell her, which led to her children getting abused. She now has her child, who has FASD, under child protection.

It's awful the bullying that she has received from them over the years from her local authority social services. A massive house and an ex-social worker herself, and now she has her daughter under child protection. It's unreal. Goes to show that it can happen to anyone. All it takes is a few malicious allegations and a social worker set on ruining a family. If only these visits were recorded and in the public eye.

I thank Amy for all her help and support and tell her that I finally have a private diagnosis. I have found some amazing people along this journey, but Amy has got to be the strongest person I have spoken to yet. I don't know how she deals with such injustice.

# Conclusion — two years later

"How's it gone?" Alan asks as I walk through the front door. Today I have been to a meeting with two councillors for our area, our MP, and around twenty ex-foster carers. Last month, the moment I never thought was coming, finally came. Marie tagged me in a post from our local news Facebook page. Children's services finally got a true reflection in their OFSTED report. They were given an inadequate rating. I was so angry to see it mentioned that children were being failed due to not having enough foster carers. *Not enough foster carers*? I typed. It's ever likely they have any at all when they treat them so badly. Once I started typing, I couldn't stop myself.

I rang the reporter, and he agreed to print a follow-up with my comments and thoughts on the OFSTED report. I was so shocked to see all the comments. I half expected the usual do-gooders to disagree and defend social services. Instead, hundreds of people commented on the way they, too, had been treated. These were not angry birth parents who'd had children removed either. A lot of them were ex-foster carers and other former employees. Since then, my inbox has filled up daily with some heart-breaking stories: nanas who have asked for help after taking on their grandchildren and ended up instead having them taken back into care.

Many foster carers weren't as lucky as me. One had a child for years. It was his fifth placement. One day he was taken for ice cream and never returned. Another child was removed into private care, shipped out like an out-of-fashion toy. The foster carer was heartbroken. She wanted to keep this child and give him a long-term home.

That's not all. For years I've asked myself the same questions. Were the safeguarding issues social services raised against me done maliciously, or because they didn't understand FASD? I now know I'm not alone. The same safeguarding tactics have been used on lots of other foster carers, too, especially on the ones who dare to speak out and fight the social workers poor practice like I did. One foster carer made a complaint about a social worker. The next week it was put in her fostering supervision notes by the same social worker that her house smelt of dogs. Many other foster carers had the same, some more serious than others. One had a spiteful complaint so serious from the birth family of the fostered child that social services got her husband arrested and then de-registered her and took the child.

I've also had a lot of warning messages. People tell me to be careful when speaking out openly to the papers about the local authority social workers because I don't know what they are capable of. Until now, I thought I did know what they were capable of, but some of the things that they have done are at the next level.

People are living in fear of them. Scared to speak out. Scared of losing their jobs, their kids, their lives at the hands of them. Some of these things happened recently, some before I was even fostering. It's been going on for years. I'm just glad that so many have finally come forward and spoken out. These are usually the ones who have hit rock bottom and have nothing left to lose. Many current foster carers message me and wish me well with getting justice but explain that they can't help because they have foster children they have had for years and can't put at risk. I completely understand their fear. We all know, too well, what goes on and what social services are capable of in our area.

"The MP was shocked," I reply now. None of them could believe that safeguarding powers are being abused in this way. A thought that never leaves me is what about birth mums? How many children have been wrongfully removed because of social workers fabricating safeguarding reports against their parents? A lot of these kids, of course, have needed to be removed, but if they can use safeguarding against so many foster carers like this by false information been recorded, I can't help but wonder how many mums have had a learning disability and just needed a bit of help?

We will never know, and these kids can never get their homes back now. I also started a petition last week to have all social services wearing body cams just like

144

the police. I used to think recording meetings was enough, but some foster carers have even had allegations of standing too close to social workers. Social workers saying they were afraid of their lives by their body language.

It's always convenient just after someone dares to stand up to them. To simply advocate for the defenceless child. We have come a long way in these past few years. I can never go back to working with children. Not just because of the record they have given me, but because I can't bear to work anywhere near them. Instead, I decided to start a new career altogether. Just last month, I got accepted into the police specials.

Hopefully, one day I will have more time on my hands to do it full-time as a paid job, but for now, I've had to put it on hold. I'm three months pregnant. Chase is going to be that middle child that they didn't want him to be. I do worry. When I went to meet my midwife, she asked me if I had ever been under social services. I said no.

I said I had been under them as a foster carer working for them and hoped they would not contact them. Every day I wake up panicking that they will use this baby to get at me to finally finish what they started. People often ask me if I knew then what I know now, would I have still had Chase. It's a very tough question I cannot simply answer.

I mean, who would choose not only to take on a child with a serious condition that the doctors aren't even trained in but also to get insulted for it. To have to give up work. To not be able to leave the house without two of you. To put your kids at risk by the powers of social services. But love is love. I love Chase more than life itself, just like I love Debbie, so I could never make any other choice but to simply keep on fighting for him.

Social services are not the only ones that anger me. I often lay awake at night wondering how many other children are out there living with FASD. How many diagnoses have been missed? I see so many clear FASD cases on disability pages. They are always diagnosed with ADHD and Autism, and several other conditions despite clear FASD facial features. Many nurses and social workers still ask me what FASD is. It's bigger and can be severer than Autism alone for goodness' sake. When is the UK going to start to acknowledge this condition?

One study found that seventy per cent of children in the care system could be affected by this, yet social services and doctors will not acknowledge it.

Being accepted into the police isn't my only success this year. I now run a FASD support group in our city. I meet up with parents and adopters once a month for a chat, to listen to their stress and offer them help. I've also put together a training course for FASD that I hope to go into schools, social services departments, and hospitals to deliver. One day I hope FASD will be out there just like Autism and ADHD. One day I hope to mention it and get, "Oh, FASD!" rather than "What is that?"

I've spoken to many birth mums of children with FASD. I don't blame them. I simply admire them. I admire them for their honesty, and I admire their acceptance and bravery. There will be thousands out there who just don't realize what diagnosis their child has because who doesn't have one drink at Christmas? Who finds out they are pregnant before going out for a drink?

I often ask people if a small glass of wine is okay to give a two-month-old. Their expression is priceless. Of course, it's not okay, so why give it to a baby that's not even formed yet? Everything a mum consumes crosses the placenta and goes straight to the baby.

My phone rings, distracting me from my thoughts. An unknown number comes up on my screen. My heart begins to race as I pluck up the courage to answer it.

"Hello, this is Beth calling from children's services." My face goes white. My hands start to shake. "We are in court today. I don't know if you are aware, but Chase has a baby brother now, and we are just checking to see if you had any intention of applying for him?"

I breathe a sigh of relief. "I can't do that," I reply. "After all, that would make Chase a middle child!"

Printed in Great Britain
by Amazon